Hawaiian Lomilomi

Aloha Patti

Mahalo nui loa for
joining us at lomilomi!
Ka lei aloha i na
Kupuna ♡

Aug 2016

﹌

With a New Foreword

by Maka'ala Yates, DC

Hawaiian Lomilomi

BIG ISLAND MASSAGE

SECOND EDITION

Nancy S. Kahalewai, LMT

I. M. PUBLISHING · MOUNTAIN VIEW, HAWAI‘I

Cover design by Pagecrafters.

Nancy S Kahalewai, LMT
www.HowToLomilomi.com
NCBTMB CE Provider # 1135

www.islandmoonlight.com

To contact the author, please e-mail: mail@bigislandmassage.com

or visit: www.bigislandmassage.com

NOTICE: *Hawaiian Lomilomi: Big Island Massage* is a reference book in a traditional
Hawaiian healing art. In your pursuit of well-being, especially if you are ill, you may
need the services of a qualified health provider who understands your needs.
The information in this book is not intended as a substitute for those services,
nor for any treatment prescribed by your personal physician.

Publisher's Cataloging-in-Publication
Kahalewai, Nancy S.
    Hawaiian Lomilomi : Big Island massage / Nancy S.
Kahalewai. — 2nd ed.
    p. cm.
    Includes bibliographical references and index.
    LCCN 2002108908
    ISBN 0-9677253-2-1

    1. Massage—Hawaii—Hawaii Island. 2. Massage
therapy—Hawaii—Hawaii Island. 3. Spiritual healing—
Hawaii—Hawaii Island.   I. Title.

RM721.K34 2003   615.8'22
                                   QB102-200701

Printed in the United States of America

This second edition is lovingly dedicated
to my *moʻopuna* (granddaughter),

Angelica Kamakanaokalani Auwae Kahalewai.

May you continue to be the gift from heaven,
which you are indeed.

Contents

Lomilomi is an ancient Hawaiian concept of working with the *mana* (life force) of the body, mind, and soul of an individual. In the old days, each village in each district on each island had its own *lomilomi* masters whom the villagers relied on and trusted.

The training to become a *lomilomi* practitioner took years. A new student was not allowed to touch a patient for three or more years, depending on his or her ability to grasp the many concepts of *lomilomi.* The student's ability to be *pono* (aligned and conflict-free) with himself or herself and to others (or to a place or thing) was also a determining factor.

The concepts of *lomilomi* are vast and complex yet simple if you understand the mechanism, principles, and intentions behind this revered form of traditional Hawaiian healing. For example, the concept of "communicating down to the bones" physically and energetically is significant because it helps the patient[1] allow the practitioner to go as deeply as the patient can tolerate, yet be noninvasive while achieving the desired results.

To obtain the level of immediate and long-term healing necessary, the practitioner uses a multitude of techniques that also affect the Golgi tendon organ (GTO) apparatus in conjunction with the muscle-spindle fiber mechanism, resulting in a quick response from the specific muscle group being worked on. The ability to communicate deep "into the bones" via the muscles and soft tissues is important because it is at this level that all memory is stored from past traumas, injuries, or emotional links. As in many indigenous cultures, the bones are the most important and protected part of both the physical structure and the energetics of the individual. It is here that specific codes are stored that make up each individual on the DNA level. Tapping into the bones allows the *lomilomi* practitioner to communicate on a soul level so that divine healing can take place.

Events in Hawai'i's history contributed to the different perceptions of and approaches to *lomilomi*. I call these reference points a "time line" of significant turning points. When the Tahitian chief and warrior Pā'ao came to the Hawaiian Islands in AD 400 or so, he forced both a class and belief system on the peaceful inhabitants. Later in the 1800s, the de facto government in Hawai'i (the illegal overthrow of the Kingdom of Hawai'i) further forced the original practitioners not to practice "sorcery," which included *lomilomi*. These actions—and many subsequent ones—attempted to suppress and change the attitudes and beliefs of the (now diluted)[2] traditional people of Hawai'i. Nonetheless, the secrets of *lomilomi* persevered through the ages in hidden formats.

Today *lomilomi* has literally reached the other side of the world and back to Hawai'i. In the right hands, it can have profound results, but the mind and heart must be open to all possibilities of healing, no matter what culture you come from.

MAKA'ALA YATES, DC

PREFACE

Lomilomi. The very word seems to have a power of its own. Perhaps sensing the unique and ancient nature of Hawaiian *lomilomi*, intrigued by the ancient stories, or curious due to a general lack of information, people are fascinated with the idea of it. There's an almost magical intrigue about both the name and spirit of *lomilomi*, sometimes called *lomi* or *lomi-lomi*, which captures aspiring as well as experienced massage therapists. Today it has become hugely popular, even almost exploited. I have received inquiries from across the United States and from as far away as Australia and Europe asking, "What exactly is *lomilomi*? How is it different from or similar to other styles? I've heard of it—where can I learn more?"

Until the first edition of this book was published in 2000, there was only one other book on the subject of *lomilomi* ever published. Titled *Lomi-Lomi Hawaiian Massage,* by Paul A. Lawrence, it is no longer in print. A few articles, training manuals, and booklets have been written, several videos have been released, and many good books on Hawaiian herbs, mythology, and shamanism are available. But still there is much confusion about what *lomilomi* is and is not. Although no book or video on massage could ever replace the person-to-person learning experience, I can certainly attempt to give the reader a thorough definition of the subject within these pages.

Writing this book has been an ongoing project. Elders have passed away and new teachers have begun teaching or sharing. I have added an index and several new chapters, and the hands-on photos in chapter 5 have all been updated. The historical and cultural information I have gathered over the years has come from many sources, sometimes conflicting, in both academic and grassroots arenas. Many native Hawaiian contributors have had no formal education and are largely self-taught. Most have pieced together teachings of their elders, their own ideas, and personal experiences. What few old records exist in the Bernice P. Bishop Museum and other archives were written in the twentieth century, mostly by non-Hawaiians about their observations and experiences of the Hawaiians doing *lomilomi*. Old records in the Hawaiian language are few and far between, and there are many nuances and layers in the Hawaiian language that have been greatly diluted or misinterpreted. This has led to many confusing or inauthentic representations of this sacred healing art that have been taken at face value by innocent and earnest seekers.

One thing is certain: *lomilomi* is much more than massage. Consequently, I have included some discussion on the Hawaiian culture and language, from which *lomilomi* cannot be separated. If you are not familiar with the correct pronunciation of Hawaiian words, or if you are new to massage therapy and plan to practice any of these techniques, I urge you to reference the section titled "A Note on Hawaiian Language," the anatomy material presented in appendix A, and the glossary.

My journey to document, interview, and research the elders and Big Island[3] healing arts officially began in 1996, but my experiential training began back in 1975. Integrating my *lomilomi* experiences with my strong background in athletic massage and anatomy has been a challenge. As a massage instructor for decades, my approach to massage therapy has been strongly analytical and intellectual—the exact opposite of most Hawaiian *lomilomi* practitioners. Gradually, I learned to experience it without analyzing it—living and breathing *aloha,* visualizing only the desired outcome, unconditionally honoring the essence of life, light, and love. During a *lomilomi* session, one must bring this presence of mind and heart to the work, and remember that each and every person is solely responsible for his or her life journey.

The light-heartedness of the elders is inspirational. They display an effortless confidence, often smiling or joking about life in general as they do their healing work. Truly a right-brained art, *lomilomi* employs a good deal of intuition as well as the healing energies of the *'āina* (the land; Mother Earth). The connection between the Hawaiians and the *'āina* is very important. This is their source of power and survival, and they know it.

Then there is the miracle of Hawai'i itself—that energy that touches your soul and draws you back to these islands again and again. That heavenly feeling we call "paradise" permeates *lomilomi.* To really experience it, you need to slow your mind's chatter, allow your senses to fully awaken and celebrate life's wonders, and then release and surrender completely.

Today there is a whole new generation of *lomilomi* practitioners joining the ranks of more than 5,000 Hawai'i-licensed massage therapists (LMTs) and a considerable number of practitioners on the US West Coast. Some styles of *lomilomi* and Hawaiian healing have spread across the United States and into Canada, Australia, Europe, and, more recently, Japan. The most widespread traditional methods have come from two great and loving native Hawaiians who were teaching way before *lomilomi* became popular: Aunty Margaret Machado, LMT, of Kona, and Uncle Kalua Kaiahua, of Maui. Other versions of Hawaiian healing arts termed "temple bodywork" and "Hawaiian shamanism" come from Abraham Kawai'i DeCambra and Serge Kahili King's teachings from Kaua'i.

There are also a handful of *kūpuna* (elders) and a few *kāhuna* (masters) quietly practicing their healing arts throughout the Hawaiian Islands in their homes, full of memories and wisdom shared only with the immediate family or *'ohana nui* (extended family). What once was kept secret or placed in *kapu* (off limits, forbidden, taboo) is slowly but surely being shared with "foreigners," and the elders are speaking openly more and more. They want this knowledge to encircle the planet, leaving a legacy for all who are ready.

I feel extremely blessed to be so embraced by the local culture and Hawaiian people. Arriving from Los Angeles in 1973, I fell in love with the islands instantly. But it took many years to feel fully comfortable in a group of local people, much less write about their healing arts. I remember feeling their sadness when Hawaiian activist George Helm "disappeared" in waters off Kaho'olawe during the early days of protesting the US bombing of that little island off the west coast of Maui, and their extreme joy when seeing the *Hōkūle'a*[4] sail into Hawaiian harbors back in 1976. The successful return from Tahiti of this double-hulled voyaging canoe, which was celestially navigated through Polynesia in the manner of the ancient ones, opened a new chapter in Hawaiian history that some refer to as the "Hawaiian Renaissance." In the mid-1970s, indigenous Hawaiians finally began to enjoy reconnecting with their proud heritage and precious *'āina* after having it literally stolen from them by self-serving foreigners. Almost overnight, bumper stickers and songs declared "Proud to be Hawaiian." Immersion elementary schools conducting all their classes in the Hawaiian language sprouted up. The "dead" Hawaiian language became the state's other official language after having been vigorously banned for several generations.

Although the last 25 years have brought a return of their culture and arts, Hawaiians are still struggling for autonomy. Most practitioners of *lomilomi* and *lā'au lapa'au* (herbal medicine) are still not allowed to practice at all. Under current laws, they cannot practice massage or herbal medicine for compensation or barter without a state license, and they can teach massage only after being licensed for at least three years. Most natives, especially the elders, are unable or unwilling to submit to the hundreds of hours of formal schooling and state exams necessary to become legally-licensed massage therapists. They have little, if any, academic training in anatomy and physiology. Many are using the same techniques they were taught by their grandparents and *kumu* (teachers) decades ago. They never did understand the "whys" of a lot of the Hawaiian healing arts, but they respectfully practice as they were taught. They regard current laws as foreign impositions. They have witnessed their heritage almost die out, their herbal medicines replaced, their lifestyles modernized, their economy disrupted by foreign investors, their lands seized by the US government, and their country overturned by annexation against democratic majority vote.

The details of what happened during the 1893 unlawful overthrow of the Kingdom of Hawai'i are now resurfacing. While the state and federal governments pay millions of dollars to administer "benefits" to the people, the natives are growing increasingly dependent and apathetic. Some are challenging all "race-based" benefits as unconstitutional, based on antidiscrimination laws. However divided, many *kānaka maoli* (native-blooded Polynesians) feel injustice and sadness deeply within their bones at the fate of their magnificent kingdom.

Understandably, most *kānaka maoli* have not yet shaken this deep resentment at having their lands and culture stolen. They are foreigners in their own home, not trusting the motives of non-natives. They were pressured to be "modern," to not succumb to the fearful practices during the *kapu* system, and to not "keep back" the *keiki* (children) from the modern ways. Now they savor their memories of the old days and ways and desperately yearn to reconnect and relearn their culture.

Until fairly recently, most *lomilomi* and herbal practitioners chose to only offer their services by word-of-mouth, simply accepting donations or bartering. Their work focused on the spiritual aspect of the healing arts, and their popularity relied purely on skill and reputation. They rarely marketed their skills, taught in business settings, or had Web sites like we see today. Most regarded healing as a sacred gift. They believed love, prayers, and *aloha* should not be for sale. But over time, things changed. A growing number of seekers, hungry for this knowledge, and the fact that the current generation of elders is passing away have left the door open for widespread, modern adaptations of *lomilomi*—sometimes exploited by unscrupulous but successful opportunists (both foreign and native).

Hawai'i has had a massage-licensing law since the 1960s. As of early 2004, the state minimum educational requirements include 50 hours of anatomy, 100 hours of the theory and practice of massage, and 420 hours of advanced training in a school or as an apprentice, closely supervised by a licensed teacher or "sponsoring" therapist. Only then can one take the licensing exam. Although Hawai'i's massage regulations fall within the US national average range of 500 hours of massage education, which is considered a good foundation to assure basic competency, it seems unrealistic to require *nā kūpuna* to comply. How do you tell a family that what has worked for many generations is now illegal, or that the *kūpuna* must stop teaching unless they have been state-licensed for three or more years, or that these elders must study anatomy and become apprentices themselves for six to twelve months? How would the state keep the patients away, stop the bartering with fruit and fish, prevent talking about the old ways? How do you discourage people from observing elders traditionally massaging those in need, just because they are not in a state-licensed clinic?

Although a dark cloud still hovers over the Hawaiians, throughout the islands there prevails a deep respect for the old ways and *'ohana* concept. Thus, in practice, the law tends to ignore those practicing traditional healing unless there is a complaint. Most households or neighborhoods have an "uncle" or "aunty" (not necessarily blood-related) who does massage or works with herbs. In the 1980s, the state legislature successfully closed most escort-massage and out-call services (prevalent in Honolulu) and cracked down on internship abuses. But unlicensed locals practicing the old methods of massage and *lā'au lapa'au* were not affected. Largely unopposed by residents and officials alike, these healers were often regarded as national treasures. Now a whole new generation of their students has risen up to carry on, some of whom are profiled in this second edition.

The licensing and education of massage therapists can provide an invaluable journey of personal growth, revelations about the functions of the human body, the perfection of safe and effective techniques, guidelines for professionalism and consumer safety, and a sound foundation for becoming part of the increasingly holistic health-care system. Yet human nature being what it is, there are also many who use the relaxed interpretation of Hawai'i massage laws as an excuse not to go to massage schools or take responsibility for sufficient training. And away from Hawaiian shores, others are teaching all sorts of non-Hawaiian things that they claim are Hawaiian. I encourage each and every reader to use discretion when learning or receiving *lomilomi*. Never feel intimidated to speak up or inquire if something does not feel right. Learn from more than one teacher. And don't be fooled into thinking that you need to pay a lot of money or dues to anyone who insists that their teachings are the best or only true teachings! For I tell you truly, this is not the Hawaiian way.

In old Hawai'i, apprentices would study for decades or a lifetime to achieve *kahuna* status. The entire community provided a sort of checks and balances against improper behavior or practice. Students of the Hawaiian healing arts should be familiar with and very respectful of the Hawaiian culture. This is the proper and most accurate way to experience and share Hawaiian knowledge and practices.

While I am very much in favor of formal massage education and taking the profession of massage to the highest level possible, I also believe that somehow the generations of tradition, intuition, and experience within the Hawaiian community must be honored. Perhaps someday soon there will be a state statute allowing certain individuals to practice their lineage of traditional Hawaiian healing safely, legally, and proudly, thus perpetuating the rich culture of Hawai'i *nei* (this beloved Hawai'i).

If you do seek out information from a *kumu*, *kupuna*, or *kahuna* (teacher, elder, or master), remember to be humble! Take a gift, and leave your expectations at home. Use discernment, and trust your intuition. And if during your visit you think you're not learning much, just be patient and observe with an open heart. If your motives are pure and you have truly given thanks, the doors will be opened and the lessons will be realized.

Acknowledgments

With deepest gratitude I honor the Big Island of Hawai'i, my home for three decades and my constant source of inspiration. Sacred is this *'āina*, with her peaks reaching into the heavens. That I could only carry your peace and majesty in my consciousness always . . .

Mahalo to my beautiful *'ohana* in Hawai'i *nei* for just being who you are! Deepest thanks to all *nā kūpuna* for all your past and present support and blessings.

Thanks to my publishing crew, especially Ernest Rose, the most resourceful and patient marketing director in the world. A big *mahalo* to Zelda Nash, editor extraordinaire, for her assistance with the editing. *Mahalo nui loa* to Kaliko Beamer-Trapp for his insights and valuable help with the Hawaiian language, and to Aunty Nona Beamer for her ongoing encouragement in the early days of the writing of this second edition.

Heartfelt appreciation is due to my administrative assistant of many years, Paul Rambo, LMT, who helped me to help so many others, and to my assistant instructor, Daniel Albers, LMT, who brought rhythm and endurance to the *lomi* workshops over the years. Thanks to Wynelle Lau for her assistance in shooting the new photos in chapter 5, and to Kalani Oceanside Retreat for the outstanding setting.

Fondest *aloha* to Robert for his pure and steadfast character. To Aunty Mahealani and my fellow *haumāna* who helped me understand these teachings, *mālama pono*.

I'd like to again express my gratitude to Sonya Vogel, who painted an original picture of a *kahuna lomilomi* working on a Hawaiian woman, which has graced the covers of both the first and second editions.

Hawaiian quotes before each chapter are used with permission from Bishop Museum Press from the book *'ŌLELO NO 'EAU: Hawaiian Proverbs & Poetical Sayings*, by Mary Kawena Pukui.

All photos and illustrations are by the author, except:

Page 41: Pele painting by Mahealani Kuamoʻo-Henry.

Page 117: Aunty Mary photo by Cora Edmonds.

Page 118: Papa Auwae photo courtesy of Julia Auwae Dahlgren.

Pages 125 & 126: Leinaʻala and Aunty Abbie photos courtesy of Kumu Leinaʻala K. Brown-Dombrigues.

Page 130: Aunty Mahealani and Uncle Kamōʻī photos by Arlene Buklarewicz.

Page 147: Serge King photo courtesy of Serge King.

A Note on Hawaiian Language

Until the 1800s, the Hawaiian language was only spoken, not written. Sounds, chants, and movements were the means for all communications. Pronunciation was critical because intonations change the meaning of a word. With the arrival of New England missionaries in 1820, the spoken sounds were translated into 12 letters. In the 1900s the glottal stop (ʻ), called an ʻuʻina or ʻokina, was officially added to signify a separation or cutting off in sound (oʻo is pronounced like "oh-oh").

Vowels: a e i o u

Consonants: h k l m n p w ʻ

A macron or line over a vowel is called a *kahakō* and elongates the vowel sound. For plurals, instead of adding the suffix *s*, *nā* may proceed the noun. It is thus improper to add an *s* to a Hawaiian word to pluralize it. The *w* is often pronounced "vee," thus "Hawaiʻi" is often pronounced "ha-vie-ee." Pronounce Hawaiian vowels as follows:

(SHORT DURATION)	(LONGER DURATION)
a as in papa	*ā* as in calm
e as in hey	*ē* as in stay
i as the second *i* in Indian	*ī* as in free
o as in token	*ō* as in throws
u as in plume	*ū* as in soothe

Latin and Spanish have the same general vowel pronunciations. In Hawaiian, all vowels are significant, and double vowels separated with an ʻokina must be pronounced distinctly:

aʻa aʻo aʻu eʻi eʻo iʻa iʻi oʻo oʻu uʻa uʻi uʻu

"The" is written *ke* or *ka* (*nā* for plural). *Ke* or *ka* can precede all nouns, unless in plural form:

ke aloha = (the) love; *ke kuli* = the knee; *ke kauka* = the doctor; *ke kakahiaka* = the morning

ka wai = the freshwater; *ka mahina* = the moon; *ka lolo* = the brain; *ka hale* = the house

nā kūpuna = the elders or ancestors; *nā hale* = the houses

Today the Hawaiian language is taught extensively in schools, and the University of Hawaiʻi offers degree programs in Hawaiian Language and Culture. In order to modernize the language, many new Hawaiian words, such as the words for "computer" and "television," have been added. This upsets some Hawaiians, who feel the essence of the language is being compromised.

Today it is correct to write entirely in the old style or entirely with the diacritical marks. In this book, we have opted to use these marks except in certain titles and words for various reasons, or whenever the elders requested that their names be left in the original forms.

This brief introduction is included to give you a feel for the rhythm of the language and some understanding of the terms and prayers used in this book. For more information about the Hawaiian language, please contact the University of Hawaiʻi. I also would recommend the online dictionary on www.ulukau.org and *"Ka Hoʻoilina: Puke pai ʻōlelo Hawaiʻi"* (The Legacy: Journal of Hawaiian Language Source), published by Kamehameha Schools Press in association with University of Hawaiʻi Press for Alu Like.

E wehe i ka umauma i ākea.

Open out the chest that it may be spacious.

Be generous and kind to all.

·1·

Hawaiian Style

Hawai'i: A Place of Healing

It is almost impossible to understand Hawaiian *lomilomi* without first understanding a little bit about Hawai'i. What is it that fills your being when you experience a tropical sunset, taste a juicy mango, smell a sweet plumeria, or feel the ocean spray on your face? You can feel the rains coming before they arrive, and when they come they are usually warm and gentle, embraced by the earth. Hawai'i offers the sensual delights of any tropical paradise and then adds a quality of re-juvenation.

Now imagine this essence infusing every cell in your body, down to your bones. The islands' healing energies can be felt by any sensitive soul, simply by smelling the air or touching the sand. In Hawai'i we call it *mana*—the power and vitality permeating these islands. Hawai'i is rich in it, and so is *lomilomi* massage.

Hawai'i is one of the most isolated places on the planet, helping it remain relatively untouched and unpolluted. It operates in its own delicate ecosystem. It seems a bit removed in time and space. It is also raw and primal, as can be witnessed in Hawai'i Volcanoes National Park[5] when molten lava explodes into the sea. Hawai'i is the manifestation of fertility born from rock, lushness emerging from barrenness. All of this gives *lomilomi* a depth and transformational quality that sets it apart from other bodywork modalities.

If you haven't experienced these islands, try to imagine what it would be like to live and breathe truly fresh air while vibrant colors and rainbows surround you. The tradewinds caress your skin, the fragrances dance by your nose, and the sounds of nature fill your ears. The oceans are the perfect swimming temperature all year, and the beaches are made of volcanic white, black, red, or olive green sand. The coolness of the mountains, with their lush carpets and canopies of green, refreshes your spirit. The earth seems to speak to you as you open your senses to her gifts, and she listens to you as well.

All but two of the world's climates can be found in the southernmost island of Hawai'i, also known as the Orchid Island, the Big Island, or, more recently, the Healing Island. Hawai'i Island is blessed with snow atop Mauna Kea (white mountain) and Mauna Loa (long mountain) after the brief winter storms. Only a few hours away from any location are tropical rain forests, coastlines and beaches, waterfalls, or simmering volcanoes. It is from this island, my home, that I focus the contents of this book.

For many centuries, the land and ocean provided everything the Hawaiians needed, and abundantly. Food and fish sources were usually within walking distance, the ocean and mountains could always be seen, and there were no harsh winters to endure. The people of each district adapted to their unique environment, and gathering, growing, and sharing food became an integral part of daily life. Villages were small, and families were close.

The ancient ones came to know this lovely place and fertile environment as their whole reality. They were grateful to God and close to the natural spirits. Their healing arts reflect this unique and intimate connection to the 'āina (the land; Mother Earth).

It is easy to romanticize about the times and peoples of old, and using terms like "ancient" and "magical" and "sacred" have added immense commercial value to some *lomilomi* marketing strategies of today. In reality, the native Hawaiians had their strengths and weaknesses like all cultures. There were effective as well as manipulative medicinal practices, wise as well as greedy leaders, and fruitful as well as destructive customs. Nonetheless, *lomilomi* was and is a truly holistic and unique healing art that continues to offer much today.

Traditional Lifestyle

In the times before European contact, the Hawaiian people had a very healthy lifestyle. Taking advantage of the abundant rainfall, they bathed several times a day, first in *kai* (salt water) and then *wai* (freshwater). Afterward, they massaged coconut oil into their skin. Hawaiians worked hard and lived entirely off the land. They were expert horticulturists and fishermen. They raised fish in shoreline fishponds kept fresh by both the ocean and streams or springs. They enjoyed a twelve-month growing, hunting, and fishing season with very favorable conditions.

Some *kāhuna* (masters and priests) grew fresh herbs for their medicines in gardens near the *heiau ho'ola* (healing temples) and gathered other ingredients in the rain forests or on the beaches. They also kept *kukui* nuts, coconuts, and dried herbs on hand, mixing medicines in calabashes, gourds, and coconut shells. Stone pounders (such as *poi* pounders for mashing *taro*)[6] were used to crush mixtures of various roots, barks, shrubs, leaves, saps, fruits, seaweed, and ferns. Animal products might be added, including urine, fish, and small sea creatures. Minerals came from *pa'akai* (salt), *lepo 'alaea* (red clay), and *lehu* (ashes). Hot stones from the fire would heat certain medicines. Enemas and steam baths promoted internal cleansing.[7]

The people knew that food is the best medicine. During sickness, the *kahuna* would prescribe specific foods and herbs. After recovery, the patient would finish the treatment by eating other prescribed foods for a specific duration of time. These were called the *pani* (closing) foods.

By necessity, Hawaiians led a physically active lifestyle. They ate a high-fiber, low-fat diet rich in vitamins and minerals. Their abundant staples included herbs, sweet potato, fresh fruits, fish, *taro*, breadfruit, and seaweed. Eventually foreigners introduced pigs, soda pop, alcohol, Spam, artificial color, refined sugar, white rice, and other unhealthy foods into the native diet. Today Hawaiians suffer from all the common ailments found in societies that eat diets high in saturated fats, chemicals, and sugar—particularly diabetes (kidneys and hormones), cancer (immune system), substance abuse (liver), high blood pressure and heart disease (circulatory system). Too often one can see unpicked citrus fruits rotting in backyards, while grocery stores are stocked

with expensive imported foods, which are frequently pur-
chased with food stamps.

But many Hawaiians still work the ocean and land daily,
fishing, planting, and harvesting as their parents did. The
Big Island *'ohana nui* (extended family) includes many local
residents still living close to the *'āina* who are considered
"living treasures," like Uncle Robert Keliihoomalu, of
Kalapana. Uncle Robert is a classic example of everything
valued in the old Hawaiian lifestyle. As he warmly welcomes
you to his ethnobotanical garden or takes you on a tour of
nearby lava fields, you feel as though you have stepped back
in time. His *'ohana* has categorized 50 common indigenous
and endemic plants by their uses for crafts, food, and medicine. A self-described country boy, he radiates with "old-
style" *aloha*. His smile stirs your heart, and his homemade
soups and herb teas soothe your *'ōpū* (tummy or abdomen).

The devastating 1990 lava flow that buried Kalapana's
black sand beach literally went around his property. Today
his home, located on eight acres of fertile land, is a gathering place for his children and grandchildren, as well as other

Hawaiians and Hawaiians-at-heart. A religious man who was born and raised as a Catholic, he perpetuates Hawaiian values and self-sufficiency. He serves as an elected Noble of the Reinstated Lawful Government of the Hawaiian Islands. He dreams and works for truth and justice for the Hawaiian people, particularly regarding self-sufficiency, ownership of their crown lands, and sovereignty following more than 100 years of the "illegal United States occupation" of Hawaiian lands and the forceful overthrow of the Kingdom of Hawai'i. For many native Hawaiians, keeping Hawaiian lands in Hawaiian hands is a deep desire and burning issue. He teaches that what makes Hawai'i beautiful is the *aloha*—the love, sharing, and caring—and that if people *mālama* (care for) the *'āina*, then it will take care of the people in return.

A Brief History

The study of the Hawaiian culture is called "Hawaiiana," a term coined several decades ago by Aunty Nona Beamer, an educator and *kumu hula* (*hula* teacher). Knowing the history and culture of the Hawaiian people gives depth to the appreciation of *lomilomi* and understanding to their perspective on healing.

One of the most frequently asked questions today at the Bernice P. Bishop Museum[8] in Honolulu is, Where did the Hawaiian people come from? Although lacking sufficient written historical archives, most authorities agree that the origin of the Hawaiian people points to the Marquesas Islands, located 1,885 miles southeast of Hawai'i. They think the Polynesians first settled in Tonga and Samoa around 1500 BC after leaving Indonesia, and then migrated to the Marquesas and Tahiti during the first century AD. They estimate that the Marquesan voyagers sailed north to Hawai'i between AD 500 and AD 700 and that the Tahitians sailed southwest to New Zealand shortly thereafter, becoming the Maori people.

Very little is known about the ancient Hawaiian culture, but it is generally agreed that before the arrival of the Tahitian warriors in the thirteenth century, the people lived a relatively peaceful life, in harmony with nature and one another in their spacious, fertile lands. Fierce warfare may not have been as essential for survival as it was in the many clusters of islands throughout the eastern South Pacific.

Polynesian chants and stories reveal the high importance placed on family values, skills, and understanding of natural phenomena. Most history was orally recorded in mythological chants, like the famous *Kumulipo* creation chant. The words the Hawaiians used to refer to objects reveal that they saw everything as sacred and at one with spirit. Spiritual reality was their whole reality, and it provided a strong foundation for their respect for the *'āina* and one another. No one needed to covet his or her neighbors' belongings. Regarding "the people of old," author Samuel Manaiakalani Kamakau wrote, "Families governed themselves for 53 generations, and . . . no man was made chief over another." Perhaps this is speculation, human nature being what it is.

In about AD 1250, Tahitian warriors led by a powerful and ruthless chief named Pā'ao conquered and forever changed the Hawaiian culture of old. Many aspects of society intensified and degenerated. Land ownership, class systems, slaves, warfare, and *kapu* (taboo) replaced the harmonious lifestyle. The social status of individuals started to take priority over their spiritual and family values. New gods were worshipped, and warfare became prevalent. *Kapu* laws were excessive and radical at times. It is believed that many Hawaiians had to withdraw to mountain caves for shelter during the wars and hide from the cruel chiefs. Other options were to submit (becoming slaves in their own homelands) or die. The people also could escape to special places of refuge called *pu'uhonua* for safety and forgiveness.

Finally, the mighty Kamehameha the Great united the islands, ending the numerous civil wars. An elaborate system of social hierarchies and taboos kept order for the people. While much of this *kapu* period was extreme, there were also many wise laws that protected the race from short-sightedness. These included practices that prevented the exploitation of the environment in an effort to guarantee an unlimited supply of food, clean water and land, and a healthy and prosperous society. Much is known about this period, including the crafts, medicines, sciences, farming, clothing, *hula*, songs, and religious beliefs. All communications were spoken save a few petroglyphs and *tapa* (decorated tree bark cloth) prints.

Then came the Europeans, the second big wave of foreigners, bringing diseases that viciously devastated the people. Captain James Cook arrived in 1778. After centuries of healthful isolation from the epidemics of the rest of the world, venereal diseases from his sailors spread quickly, and tens of thousands of natives died. During the 1800s, whooping cough, leprosy, influenza, measles, smallpox, diphtheria, cholera, bubonic plague, and scarlet fever took a heavy toll, killing from 10 to 25 percent of the people in each successive epidemic. By 1819, tobacco and alcohol had been introduced to the Hawaiians. The *kapu* and law of the land was broken shortly thereafter, and before long European doctors and churches had replaced all the medical *kāhuna* and *heiau* (temples).

By 1850, the native population was reduced to 82,000 from about 300,000 only 75 years before. By the end of the century, Christian missionaries had for better or worse penetrated all aspects of Hawaiian culture, followed by greedy businessmen (often members of the church as well) who married into the royal families and influenced the ruling kings and queens with their political ideas. The generosity of the islanders and strategic location of the islands provided the business opportunities of a lifetime to foreign governments. It wasn't long before the Hawaiian people lost most of their native population, their beloved Queen Lili'uokalani,[9] and all of their sovereignty and crown lands.

The 1900s brought the plantations, immigrants, and eventually US statehood. In the last thirty years, thanks to events like the round-trip navigation of the *Hōkūle'a* voyaging canoe, momentum for the native culture and language has been building.

Today the native Hawaiians are a proud but all-too-often physically unhealthy people who have been trained to depend on the federal government and Western culture. But the soul and spirit of the *kānaka maoli* (native-blooded Polynesians) are still strong, and their culture is revered and respected around the world. Like their native language and *hula*, healing arts like *lomilomi* are gradually finding their way back into their daily lives and drawing interest from around the globe.

ʻIke nō i ka lā o ka ʻike;
mana nō i ka lā o ka mana.

Know in the day of knowing;

mana in the day of *mana*.

Knowledge and *mana*—each has its day.

~2~

What Is Lomilomi?

Defining the Art

Lomilomi is the traditional massage of Hawai'i developed over many generations by the people of the islands. *Lomilomi* begins and centers on a state of consciousness that reflects the grace and *aloha* of Hawai'i. It enables the physical and energetic systems of the body to flush out, transform, and revitalize as the soft tissues are gently but firmly loosened, separated, and loved. It encompasses releasing and forgiving in order to bring all aspects of self into alignment. It is holy and holistic, sacred yet practical.

The most important ingredient of *lomilomi* is a genuine and unpretentious way of being with your self, your 'āina, your 'aumākua (spirit guides or guardians), your client, and Akua (God). *Lomilomi* is the hands-on manifestation of *aloha* and unconditional love skillfully delivered into the soft tissues of the body.

Like all healing arts, *lomilomi* has evolved over the millennia. It was influenced by the Asian healing arts as well as European practices. The techniques are not difficult, yet their proper application takes years to master. By modern standards, the strokes are quite simple, many resembling deep classical European techniques.

One of the biggest misconceptions people have about *lomilomi* is that it is a specific set technique or routine. There are probably more versions of *lomilomi* than any other type of bodywork. Hawaiian *lomilomi* has as many styles as it has practitioners. All the great original practitioners did *lomilomi* differently. Each island, every extended family, each *ahupua'a* (land division from ocean to mountain), and each system of healing was unique.

As diversified as it is, *lomilomi* always encompassed body, mind, and spirit but in a different way than we see today. There were many forms of faith healing, distance or absent treatments, and kinds of exorcism and telepathy that were regularly practiced. *Lomi* included massage or bodywork, but, most important, it was a state of mind that encompassed the consciousness of both the giver and receiver. The actual massage techniques were only part of the *lomilomi* treatment, as my "*lomilomi* pie" illustrates:

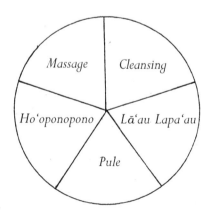

An Unwritten Art

One of the reasons *lomilomi* is so difficult to write about is because it is essentially an unwritten art. It was never nationalized (like Namikoshi's shiatsu in Japan, for example), nor was it ever put into written form.

Primarily due to the wonderful *oli* (chants) and keen memorization skills so valued by their culture, specific family traditions survived for many generations. While particular family traditions were kept amazingly intact for many generations, each lineage was kept pure and separate from the others. Medicinal recipes, the gathering and cultivation of secrets, and the knowledge of when it was *kapu* to use certain practices or substances were mastered and passed down by the *kahuna lā'au lapa'au* (herbal medicine master).

After the missionaries taught the natives how to read and write, many plant formulas and healing testimonials were written down in the Hawaiian language in journals kept by the herbalists. But in time, the de facto Department of Health of the Provisional Government discouraged and punished practitioners of the traditional arts. And many natives were understandably weary of the sometimes superstitious and dangerous ways of the *kāhuna* who would often practice sorcery or cast manipulative spells on others. Many preferred Christianity and the security of one merciful God to the harsh *kapu* system.

Learning *lomilomi* was never a textbook affair. The Hawaiian way of teaching and sharing has always been a personal gift passed from the *kumu* to a chosen student in nonwritten form. It was not a commercial venture, and there were no massage schools to attend. The "old style" method of learning is primarily done by one-on-one observation and imitation, and only after the student proves ready, worthy, and truly serious. In all the arts, whether building canoes or setting fractured bones, the designated initiates would observe their *kumu* (teacher; source) for years, then imitate the work with supervision. No books, lengthy explanations, detailed assessments, or question-and-answer periods were allowed.

Hawaiian *lomilomi* always was, and among indigenous islanders still is, considered a sacred healing art that was passed down directly and precisely from *kahuna* practitioner to a chosen younger family member. Interestingly, the initiates rarely received the work themselves, which is considered an invaluable part of learning massage today.

Yet this learning method of quiet, respectful observation is still used today, particularly in the *hālau hula* (Hawaiian dance schools). According to Maui's Kapiiohookalani Lyons Naone, a traditional Hawaiian *lā'au lapa'au* practitioner, traditional learning should follow certain protocols: *nānā* (to see with all eyes), *ho'olohe* (to listen with all ears), *hana ka lima* (using your hands), and *pa'a ka waha* (to be silent).

To the analytical Western mind, this teacher-student relationship seems unusually strict. There doesn't seem to be enough dialogue. There's no rerun button. But Hawaiians believed that students should put their full attention behind their eyes and ears: Watch what happens! Look, listen, and breathe! In time, when you are ready, you will understand.

The Hawaiian Way

In the true Hawaiian way, when *lomilomi* is given to another, it is always done so for free (or by donation), the way one would give their dearest beloved a special gift, or as the warm Hawaiian rains give life to the land. Until recent times, one would never charge another for sharing a gift from God, and all healing was regarded as a divine gift.

When the current state-licensing laws went into effect in the 1960s, only European and Oriental massage was done as a business—never *lomilomi*. Sailors and foreign businessmen made up the bulk of the customers, and a one-hour massage was about $5.00. But the locals relied on the neighborhood's elder who would pray, use special plants, and *lomi* anyone in need, free-of-charge. Gifts of appreciation (like food) would be accepted, but never money. To this day, it is also considered essential to receive a personal blessing from one's *kanaka maoli* teacher to go forth and practice or teach *lomilomi* and *lāʻau lapaʻau* as an occupation.

If you travel deep into the countryside, "free" takes on a whole new meaning. Here one can live immersed in the tropical rhythms of nature. You eat the fresh fruits in season and plant and fish in harmony with the moon. You share and trade your seasonal bounty with your neighbors. You rely on the wisdom of your elders, and eat the herbs they give you. Everyone can count on one another when in need, and no one has to go without. This *kōkua* (cooperation) method richly supplies everyone in the community with all that is needed. Charging a fee is simply unnecessary because it's not about money at all.

Today *lomilomi* has become so popular it is too often competitive. While some see it as a means to further their personal status, and the massage industry views it as a hot spa or clinic modality, I prefer to see it as an evolving traditional system that can offer the world the best of both old and new concepts. These are critical times. People seem to be experiencing an acceleration of consciousness. Many want and need more than the healing options available from allopathic and alternative health care.

The Power of *Lomilomi* Massage

While *lomilomi* can offer new perspectives in healing, in other ways it is really quite simple. Massage is one of the most basic ways to care for the body—it keeps the tissues supple, fluids moving, emotions cleared, nerves calm, and energies flowing.

In the Hawaiian tradition, purification precedes any hands-on massage, as well as most sacred endeavors. The body is cleansed physically, emotionally, and spiritually. It's just as critical to make *pono* (realign; correct) the client's self-defeating thoughts as it is to address his or her physical problems. Individual ties to any negative person, place, or thing are corrected with the help of a higher power. In traditional *lomilomi* bodywork, medicinal herbs, *ti* plants, Hawaiian salt, stones, sweat lodges, water immersion, hot rocks, and *lomi* sticks are all frequently used as healing tools.

In midwifery, *lomilomi* was used to turn breech babies and ease the birthing process. The women would assume a supported squatting position while the upper abdomen was carefully massaged with *kukui* nut oil with a downward pressure. Afterward, *lomi* was gently applied to mold the features (head, hands, back, hips, and limbs) of the young child.

Sometimes *lomilomi* was done simply to reduce discomfort. Many references found in the Bishop Museum archives describe the benefits as witnessed and recorded by foreigners. These included relief from overeating, headaches, fatigue, and general pains. Some writings from 1775 noted, "The *aliʻi* . . . had servants to fan the flies and to massage them." W. D. Alexander wrote of the attendants of the royalty: "One to hold the *kāhili* fly-brush, another in charge of his spittoon, and another who sat ready to *lomilomi* whenever desired." In the late 1830s, James Jarves told of an old Kauaʻi chief who "submits his body to the manipulation of two aged but skillful women." Charles Nordhoff, who visited the islands in the 1870s, wrote that "to be lomi-lomied, you lie down upon a mat, loosen your clothing or undress for the night, if you prefer. The less clothing you have on, the more perfectly the operation can be performed. To you thereupon comes a stout native, with soft fleshy hands but a strong grip, and the whole body seizes and sqeezes [*sic*] with a quite peculiar art," and every tired muscle is "worked and kneaded with indefatigable patience."

In 1939 there are references to "walking massage" by practitioners "supporting their weight with heavy sticks or rods" as they massaged the fleshy areas with their feet. All written references generally agree that the practice was very lulling and pleasing when gently performed, and that after the thumping, pounding, squeezing, and pinching, a pleasant relaxation and sleep followed. Some practitioners still practice *lomilomi* on a mat on the floor, no doubt the way it was done before tables were introduced.

The temple bodywork styles so prevalent today refer to the body being a sacred temple of the soul. Some movements resemble *lua*, the martial arts of the *kāne* (men). At one point, in fact, these powerful meditative arts of the *kāne* had to go underground, and soon found expression in the *hula* as performed by the men. Many hand and foot movements of *lua* can be found in temple bodywork, which "dances" around the table. Although the ancient forms of *lomi* (or *romi* as it is called in the South Pacific) were done with the hands and feet while the patient would lie on a woven mat on the ground, this bodywork is done on a massage table with one or two practitioners who use big horizontal movements with their forearms to move energy. The energy work behind this style of modern bodywork comes from ancient teachings of personal empowerment, as required during *hula* and martial arts performances, and was taught in the *heiau*. Although the pressure is not as deep as traditional *lomi*, people report tremendous benefits after receiving this style of bodywork, which is discussed in more detail in chapter 8.

Traditional *lomi* dramatically improves circulation of body fluids, which brings oxygen and nutrients to the cells while removing metabolic wastes. Composed of many gliding and kneading strokes, it has the same benefits as Swedish massage, primarily affecting the circulatory, nervous, and musculoskeletal systems.

Whether traditional, modern, or temple in origin, *lomilomi* certainly induces profound physiological changes. The full-body routines as practiced today are rhythmic. The moves are both invigorating and soothing. The breath is deep. The attitude is loving and reverent. Ideally, the hands are "soft like clouds" yet the pressure is firm. The session is a "right-brained" experience as both the therapist and receiver are deeply blessed and often transported into an altered state. In the end, that wonderful post-massage feeling of nurtured peace lingers, opening the door for renewal, restoration, and trans-formation.

Effects and Contraindications

Massage increases the client's awareness in the areas being massaged, and awareness in itself can help bring about healing. Massage is an excellent way of communicating nurturing, love, and trust. Massage balances the flow of vital life energy within the client and creates an exchange of vital energy between the therapist and client. During a massage, the client is offered the chance to be totally nurtured and supported by the therapist. This provides an opportunity to let go of the accumulated tensions that are part of daily life. By releasing chronically held physical tension, the corresponding emotional component can surface and be released. Massage is also one of the nicest ways to bond or share with another in an intimate relationship (between partners and in families). In addition, massage provides specific physiological benefits:

- **Circulatory.** Massage acts to dilate the blood vessels, which increases the efficiency and supply of fresh nutrients to the tissues and eliminates metabolic wastes from the body. Kneading and gliding strokes promote the venous return of blood back toward the heart, which is particularly beneficial to enhance proper circulation within the extremities. Massage acts as a mechanical cleanser, helping to drain sluggish lymph material. Good lymphatic circulation is important for ridding the body of toxins and enhancing immunity.

- **Musculoskeletal.** Massage stretches and relaxes tight, tense muscles. Massage (especially transverse strokes) helps to prevent adhesions from occurring in between the muscle fibers. When muscle fibers adhere together, full range of motion is restricted. Massage stretches the connective tissue, which surrounds and supports the musculature, thus promoting its health and preventing it from adhering to the muscle. Massage can help to lessen the stiffness and swelling found within the joints. It improves muscle tone by mechanically stimulating inherent reflexes found within muscle fibers. This is helpful for those who do not obtain adequate daily exercise due to sedentary lifestyles.

- **Nervous.** Massage is a terrific stress-buster. It can have either a stimulating or sedative effect on the nervous system depending on the type of massage given, the duration of actual massage time, and the present state of the nervous system. It can "reprogram" neurological patterns and greatly reduce pain, emotional armoring, and impaired sensations. Some techniques can improve motor-nerve function to organs and muscles, thus helping their functional capacity.

- **Internal organs.** Massage on the abdomen aids digestive and eliminative channels to improve function and efficiency of the internal organs and gastrointestinal tract. It can also help in pregnancy or in restoring proper location of certain organs. These areas have always been emphasized in *lomilomi*.

- **Skin.** Massage aids the function of both the oil and sweat glands in the skin, our largest organ. It soothes the tens of thousands of nerve endings and flushes out miles of small capillaries. Certain techniques exfoliate dead skin cells and keep the skin healthy.

Contraindications are situations in which massage may make conditions worse. This is a brief overview of common ones. In general, they can be divided into two types:

1. **Caution necessary.** There are times when a massage is inadvisable. It may be necessary to avoid a particular area or abstain from using certain massage techniques, which may cause damage. Sometimes one can massage around the injury, for example, by staying on healthy tissue only. At other times, one can do light work or energy work, while avoiding other strokes that will only irritate the condition.

   Caution is necessary for: burns and sunburn, joint pathologies, tumors and cysts, bruises, acute sprains and strains, cuts and abrasions, herpes and shingles, swelling and inflammation, skin rashes and diseases, neuralgia, osteoporosis, pregnancy, hypersensitivity, post-surgery recovery, edema, post-event or extreme overuse, diabetes, and degenerated tissues (especially joints). Please make sure you study pathologies in order to avoid accidentally injuring your clients.

2. **Total abstinence.** In some cases, it is best not to massage at all. Consulting a skilled physician can be a wise choice if you suspect any possible serious condition. The client may be rescheduled for another session, referred to a specialist, or asked to return after the condition subsides. It is always best to be safe so as to protect both the recipient and practitioner.

   These contraindications include: all contagious diseases, fever, extreme intoxication, phlebitis, blood clots, severe circulatory diseases, fractures, acute injuries or dislocations, severe systemic pathologies, and cancer (unless the client's physician approves).

He ʻonipaʻa ka ʻoiaʻiʻo.

Truth is not changeable.

❦ 3 ❧

The Body

The Hawaiian Holistic View

The ancient Hawaiians had a very holistic view of the body and its interrelated levels of consciousness. They concentrated on the vital life forces in their healing arts. They saw everything as being alive energetically, including nonliving matter. After sufficient cleansing and purification, they believed most diseases could improve under the right conditions. They knew that even the densest parts in the body, like the bones, were living tissues and thus could heal. They practiced adjustments to biomechanically align the joints, essential in the martial arts.

Perhaps they did not know that blood cells originated in bone marrow, but they knew that the bones contained the essence of the individual's personal *mana* and ancestral lineage. They realized that the body was a temporary vehicle for the spirit while on the earth journey, and they believed that there was life after life. They carefully tended to the bones of the dead, particularly if the deceased was a chief or chiefess.

Legends tell of Hawaiian women who regularly tended to the dead chiefesses, who were often consecrated and deified. The body would be cleansed, massaged with fine oil, and perfumed with flowers during a purification ritual. Gifts were given and the attending women would *oli* (chant) about her glory and beauty. Then they would mourn by singing and wailing her attributes. For about ten days, they would have a ceremony as they helped the dying process of fading away from this dimension to the next. The remains would be cooked in a shallow *imu* (earth oven) so that bleeding and rotting would no longer defile her. Then they would separate her flesh from her bones. The bones would be wrapped in *kapa* cloth and buried in a deep cave. Sometimes the flesh would be bundled up and reverently taken to either the volcano (Pele clan), a river or cave (*moʻo* lizard clan), or thrown into the ocean for the sharks (*manō* clan), depending to which *ʻaumakua* the family or clan belonged.

High-ranking or deeply loved and respected men were also treated after death with great ceremony. Their bodies might be baked in the *imu* to help the flesh fall off the bones. Certain bones would then be wrapped or used in special baskets, weapons, or other personal items. Sometimes bodies were left in their final, well-hidden resting places whole, as full skeletons found curled up in fetal positions or lying under canoe hulls suggest.

In addition to the wonderful insights they had into the mysteries of life and death, there were many primitive and superstitious practices as well. Especially during the time of the radical *kapu* practices, fear of breaking a *kapu* or manipulation from a vengeful spirit or *kahuna* was part of daily life. During the times when Kū was the main God[10] being worshipped, human sacrifices were performed and death was a frequent fate of wrongdoers; during the times when Lono prevailed, harmony returned. As recently as a few generations ago, Hawaiians were extremely careful not to leave behind their cut hair or any personal item for fear that an ill-wishing person or *kahuna* may find and use it against them or their families.

In healing, the body-mind connection (so popular in massage therapy today) was always part of the intention of the *kāhuna*. They never conceived of separating body and mind—or any other part of a person. The Western concept of the body as a great machine was never part of their belief system. Patients were assessed holistically. The condition of the physique was not separated from that of the psyche. If one had indigestion, for example, the *kahuna* would inquire as to what was going on with the "gut feelings" as well as check if there was anything done to or by the patient to bring this about.

In *lomilomi*, as with all bodywork, understanding anatomy and kinesiology greatly aids the therapist in giving an effective and specific massage. It is also important to develop the art of palpation, something at which the Hawaiians excelled. Beyond the physical pains and biomechanics of the individual, they usually worked on balancing and healing four primary body-mind centers. These have distinct qualities and form the Hawaiian holistic perspective that opens the way to deeper healing:

1. **Na'au** (gut instincts). This center, located in the abdomen, can be counted on to give you reliable and accurate feedback. When deep in your belly you feel

something is not right, it isn't. The *na'au* functions as the keeper of the body. It's always direct and dependable, and in the present moment.

2. **Pu'uwai** (the heart center). The heart governs the emotional aspect of human existence. While the heart is the center for compassion and *aloha*, it is also the center for foolishness and sorrow. Yet the highest and most effective place from which to treat others is from the *pu'uwai*, even when the person does not seem receptive to it. We can know something in our heart, but we should trust our *na'au*.

3. **Mana'o** (the intellect). Your thoughts determine your reality. They lead the way for your emotions. You can rationalize and analyze to gain better understanding, but the mind can get stuck in excessive, random thinking. Successful people choose to reprogram their intellect with mindful thoughts that bring harmony between all the centers.

4. **Mauli ola** (spiritual being). Spirit is your true sacred identity, and the body is its temporal package. Perfection, righteousness, and correct living is achieved when we identify with the divine, or our higher self, and then align our human nature with it. Spirit is eternal, but the human experience is temporary. God dwells within you, speaking to you through your unconditionally loving thoughts, if you are receptive. Claim your true identity, and all things are possible.

For some fascinating research, I recommend a visit to the Bishop Museum archives in Honolulu. You can find old documents describing hundreds of pathologies and diseases, their corresponding Hawaiian treatments, and medicinal uses of foods, herbs, animal substances, minerals, hydrotherapy, hot stones, enemas, and basic surgery. The Bishop Museum has published comprehensive, historical reports on Hawaiian anatomical and physiological terms and detailed treatments, including herbal pharmaceuticals (see Bulletin #126 written in 1934). For more on the subject of Hawaiian medicines, please see chapter 6.

Mana: Your Personal Power

Mana is the vital universal force manifest in you. Called *chi, ki,* or *prana* in Asia, *mana* represents the vital energy of all phenomena and life. This energy constantly flows throughout all of creation. Beyond biological forms, *mana* refers to the energetic levels of atoms and electrons as well. You need sufficient *mana* to maintain good health, good relationships, and a healthy attitude. When you are low in *mana* you are more vulnerable and prone to illness. In order to effectively do bodywork on another, you need to have sufficient *mana.* If you do not, you are much more susceptible to the transference of energies, including absorbing your client's unbalanced energies.

Hawaiians have always felt that some objects and life forms have more *mana* than others, but that all things have *mana,* including the mountains and rocks. They also believed that some lineages carried more ancestral *mana* than others. Their culture was based on beliefs that the blood of some people had more *mana* than others, leading to inbreeding within the royal families. In *Mana Cards: the Power of Hawaiian Wisdom,* author Catherine Kalama Becker states that the *ali'i nui* (kings or queens) "were believed to possess so much *mana* that they could intercede between the people and nature. They also believed their *mana* could be stolen from them through sorcery or if someone walked on their shadow."

Mana also refers to an individual's personal power. It does not refer to mere talent, charisma, charm, or sweetness. It is *power.* Samuel Kamakau wrote, "Solid rocks were melted away by the *mana* of the prayers." Author Mary Kawena Pukui described it as an "inherent quality of command and leadership . . . a reservoir of strength." Pali Jae Lee wrote, "Many want *mana,* but few will pay the price. The price is high, but so are the rewards." Lee also noted, "When real and great *mana* is achieved, the person is probably no longer looking for it." Lee is referring to the deepest substance within great individuals who have evolved past their ego. In this state of consciousness, they have become masters through years of hard work, experience, and learning. "There was no longer a line between them as a person and what they did."

Although *mana* is found in all things, most Hawaiians get their personal *mana* from the elements of nature, particularly from the earth itself. In this sense, it is very grounding.

Greg Scott, author of *Pacific Voyager Cards,* has studied Western psychology as well as how to develop *mana* with several Hawaiian *kāhuna.* He points out that any conscious action increases our *mana.* "Anything done with presence, where there is an action and a 'you' doing the action consciously, builds *mana.*" *Mana* relies on awareness and attention, so be mindful of what you do and how you do it. *Mana* moves on attention, so pay attention. Since everything you do requires *mana,* spend it wisely.

Sufficient *mana* is essential in *lomilomi* massage. Hawaiian bodywork, like almost every quality of these beautiful islands, is known for its high degree of life-enhancing, transformational *mana*. Scott teaches that the first step in developing *mana* is recognizing and avoiding things that leak or drain *mana:*

- **Physical.** Physical leaks include obvious stresses and excess tension. Inactivity also causes the body to suffer and become weaker. Don't get caught up in frequently being in a hurry or rushing from one task to another. Don't be self-abusive by continuously eating poorly, smoking excessively, or consuming too much alcohol, caffeine, or drugs.

- **Emotional.** Our emotions affect our *mana* more than our physical bodies do. One fit of anger can drain us of several day's worth of *mana*. Letting sadness, worry, fear, anger, resentment, and self-pity run rampant can drain us completely. Many emotions, although "negative," may be an appropriate response. However, blocking them, pretending they don't exist, or holding on to them too long can have drastic effects. Neediness is another emotional leak. Notice how much maneuvering one does to get a compliment or to impress others. The antics we engage in for such a small return are defeating. Resentment, jealously, and constantly criticizing others rob us of any chance of developing true personal power.

- **Mental.** Some of the subtlest leaks come from our mental center. Making judgments, jumping to conclusions, and labeling others is dangerous to high levels of *mana*. Any mental excess drains our energy. Too much useless talking, daydreaming, letting our imagination run away with events that will never happen, reviewing past and future conversations over and over all require lots of energy that never gets repaid. Limiting belief systems also sabotage our lives—"I'm no good, too old, too thin, etc."—and excessive self-importance is equally defeating. Thinking we know it all, are superior, and similar self-centered ideas wastes our power.

Many leaks occur on multiple centers. With some honest self-observation it doesn't take long to see where we're feeling drained. Each action, feeling, sensation and thought is an opportunity to be filled or drained with *mana*. If you want to do more, be more, have more . . . you need more *mana*. Once we've seen our own leaks and begun to change them, we can develop our *mana* in more direct ways:

- **Physically.** In order to maintain strength and vitality, we must balance exercise and rest. Listening to our bodies about food intake and the need for sleep is important. Greg Scott suggests learning new skills, like sports, martial arts, and dancing. Stop useless nervous actions with periods of relaxation and stillness. Make extra efforts and complete any task through to its end, whether it is simple or difficult. Do your best. Spend time in nature, as the natural world radiates *mana* that you can readily use.

- **Emotionally.** To experience joy, self-acceptance, and a sense of inner peace, practice forgiveness. Go with the flow and give yourself a break. You do not have to be perfect! Accept others, as they are not perfect either. Develop trust. Take care of yourself. Spend time connecting to nature, to others, to self. How you do something is more important than what you do.

- **Mentally.** Seek out real understanding. Beyond book learning, seek direct knowledge. Study and learn new things. Develop your concentration, visualizations, and positive "self-talk." Cultivate empowering beliefs, and let go of any that drain you. What you can picture in your mind and focus on, you can create. Focus your body on excellence, your heart on trust, and your mind on observation.

Suggestions for *Lomilomi*

Before beginning a *lomilomi* session, empty yourself completely. Focus on breathing for a few moments. With each exhale, emptiness. With each inhale, *mana.* Use visualization to watch *mana* filling you. Each touch during the massage must be done with your whole being. Don't allow your mind to wander. Keep a sense of lightness and humor. Feel connected. Radiate love, acceptance, and peace. Help your client feel his or her own connection and *mana.* When finished with the session, keep clear and empty toward the client. No judgments, no expectations. Accept the results, give your client a blessing, and then let go. Remember each and every client is fully responsible for his or her own life.

Basic Anatomy

I love to say, "Everyone with a body should study basic anatomy!" Although learning anatomy wasn't stressed in ancient *lomilomi,* palpation was. Understanding certain concepts helps one appreciate the body's natural healing abilities as well as injury and disease prevention. This is true not only for those in health-care occupations but for those who live with health challenges or undue levels of stress, wear, and tear on the body.

For any massage therapist, being able to "visualize" in your mind what lies under the skin of the area you are working on and "feel" what your client is feeling as you work makes all the difference. It puts you in touch with your client on a deep kinesthetic level and makes the difference between a relaxing massage and a truly transformational one with long-lasting results. It lets you really "talk" to the body—restoring what needs to be restored, releasing what needs to be released.

If you are planning to do *lomilomi* and have never studied anatomy, the following may help you to understand the effects of massage.

Imagine that you are a big container of water—a self-contained "pond." It is up to you to keep it fresh, unpolluted, well-circulated, and pure. Otherwise, you will become stagnant and a breeding ground for pathogens.

There are five types of tissues in your pond, and they are all composed of atoms and molecules in the form of cells (the smallest unit of life forms) and "matrix" (intercellular protein and mineral tissue) in different ratios:

1. **Liquid** (blood and lymph) tissue is abundant, circulating almost everywhere in your body, bringing nutrients, oxygen, and white blood cells to fight infection and nourish you, bathing every cell and tissue to cleanse away waste matter. It is 45 percent cellular and 55 percent matrix.

2. **Nerve** tissue allows communication between every muscle, organ, gland, brain cell, and sensory part of your body, and it allows you to perceive, create, and grow in consciousness. These cells cannot reproduce as in the normal

mitosis process. The dendrites and axons of the cell can often regenerate, but once the cell body dies, it is gone forever. Other nerve cells will try to compensate, but because you have a limited number of these cells to last your entire life, function significantly declines following excessive damage.

3. **Muscle** tissue responds to neural commands, creating the movement of your heart and every healthy joint in the body. Muscle cells or fibers contain microscopic filaments that slide past each other during movement. If movement, circulation, or nerve function slows down, scar tissue or atrophy sets in, and your muscles become more fibrous and less cellular.

4. **Epithelium** is composed of layers of cells that cover and line many of your inner surfaces and your entire outer skin. This tissue is totally cellular and can perform mitosis as it heals. But scar tissue can still get in the way, as in the case of the permanent destruction of the epithelium in the delicate air sacs of your lungs from smoking.

5. **Connective** tissue is everything else—your bones, tendons, ligaments, teeth, cartilage, and strong tissue called "fascia" that wraps each organ and muscle in supportive sections, much like strong cheesecloth wrapped around fresh cheese. This is mostly matrix, with a few cells circulating about, and thus is slow to heal and dependent on scar tissue for recovery. Never overstretch damaged connective tissue the first week or so following a fresh injury or surgery, or the scar tissue will become excessively dense and irregular.

It is helpful to understand the qualities and limits of each tissue type, where each is located, and how to help the healing process. Knowing anatomy enables the massage practitioner to increase beneficial physiological effects from each massage session and understand applicable contraindications. *Never* cause injury to your client. For example, vigorous *lomilomi* is never indicated when tissue is inflamed, infected, torn, or acutely injured. But prayers and energy work may be done safely. Ice applications are also extremely beneficial at this stage.

When tissue is bound up with adhesions, too inactive or overused, or full of chronic tension, massage can be a lifesaver! It is natural to hold tension, compensation, memories, stress, and even emotions in various parts of the body. When this happens, or if you have postural asymmetry or overwork parts of your body over a long time, dysfunctions or disease processes easily occur. When your tissues do not function normally, that part of your "pond" stagnates. Blood cannot circulate, waste cannot be eliminated, muscles cannot stretch or contract efficiently, oxygen cannot revitalize the cells, and nerves cannot communicate properly. Eventually, pain and problems become serious and chronic.

It can become challenging to fix or "heal" the problem. Ideally, problems should be prevented in the first place, but once a condition exists, the massage therapist should address it responsibly or refer the client to a specialist. We must listen to the body, understand what is going on, and then take steps to undo what has caused the situation. We must find the causes of the causes and assist the client in correcting them if possible. We must refer the client to the appropriate medical specialist when the situation necessitates it.

Most underlying causes can be traced to pathogens, toxins, abuse, lack of nutrition, dysfunction, traumatic injury, genetics, or more subtle imbalances. The body, mind, and spirit are intertwined, thus the causes can be physical, mental, or emotional, and each can affect the other. It is quite empowering to experience a healing when the cause of the problem is successfully resolved. This is far superior to any Band-Aid solution or merely manipulating the current symptoms.

The current renaissance in the healing arts is largely due to the fact that individuals are expanding their perception of the possible causes, while taking more personal responsibility for their health. Natural techniques and substances that aid in the restorative properties of the cells and tissues are being increasingly utilized. The ancient uses of herbs are slowly but surely making their way into the allopathic health-care system through nutraceutical research and public demand. But many indigenous practitioners believe that wild herbs have the most *mana* and that nature is the best pharmacy if used with wisdom and proper protocol.

For reference charts on major muscles, nerves, vessels, and bones, please see appendix A.

Related Hawaiian Terms

a'a: small vessel, nerve, or fiber

hānau: to give birth

hāpai: pregnant

ho'onahā: to cause a cleansing of the bowels

'ili: skin

'i'o: flesh; muscle

iwi: a bone

kapua'i: sole of the foot

kino: body; physical

koko: blood

kuamo'o: pertaining to the backbone

lauoho: hair (of the head)

loko: inside; internal organ

lolo: brains; bone marrow

ma'i: ill

ma'i lele: contagious illness

maka: eye

nini: external balm or ointment

olonā: strong cord (ligament or tendon)

'o'opa: limping, disabled

pailua: seasickness, nausea

pana pu'uwai: heartbeat, pulse

pe'ahilima: palm of the hand

piko: crown of head; umbilical; genitals

piwa: fever

waimaka: tears

wale: phlegm, saliva

Parts of the Body

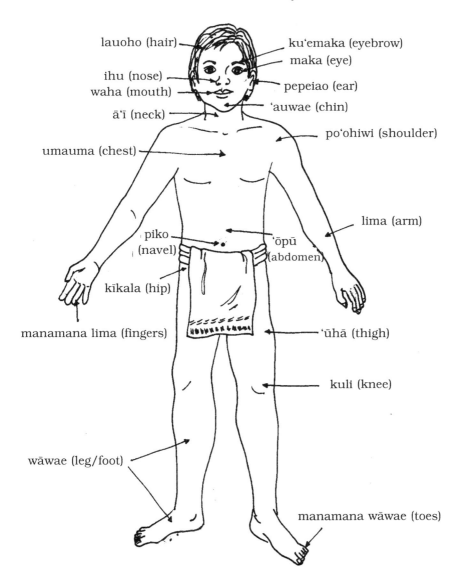

lauoho (hair)

ku'emaka (eyebrow)

maka (eye)

ihu (nose)

waha (mouth)

pepeiao (ear)

ā'ī (neck)

'auwae (chin)

po'ohiwi (shoulder)

umauma (chest)

lima (arm)

piko (navel)

'ōpū (abdomen)

kīkala (hip)

manamana lima (fingers)

'ūhā (thigh)

kuli (knee)

wāwae (leg/foot)

manamana wāwae (toes)

He kēhau ho'oma'ema'e ke aloha.

Love is like a cleansing dew.

Love removes hurt.

❖ 4 ❖

The Elements of Lomilomi

Pule

True *lomilomi* always begins with a *pule*, or prayer, silently, verbally, or as a traditional Hawaiian chant. It is always acknowledged that the healing is in the hands of God or of the recipient's higher self, which is directly connected to God. *Pule* centers the practitioner and prepares him or her to be a vehicle for loving, selfless service; it focuses the intention and invokes intuition. *Pule* also prepares the recipient to be open to the possibility of healing and to be receptive to more subtle levels of reality and awareness.

The Hawaiians knew the value of praying, sometimes for days in advance of a *lomilomi* session. Often they would not proceed until they received a "message" from Akua (God; the Supreme Being) in a dream or vision, clarifying the patient's deepest needs. A truly gifted healer can resonate with the higher frequency of the divine presence, serving as a conductor of this energy, and direct it into the body part that seems blocked or is in a state of distress. The effectiveness of this sort of connection between practitioner and patient can be so powerful that physical contact may not even be necessary. It is as if another dimension has been entered.

Before one begins a *lomilomi* session, one should be in the proper state of mind. Exercises to help "get yourself out of your way" and to increase your *mana* (energy) are beneficial. Hawaiians will often sing or chant softly as they work, putting their clients at ease as well. Filling yourself with genuine gratitude and peace is important. It is easy to feel God's presence in Hawai'i, but wherever you are, you can create that sacred feeling of being one with the Holy Spirit.

During times of peace, the ancient Hawaiians had a naturally conducive environment for this. Living on a large tropical island, eating fish, *taro*, herbs, and fruits, they worked closely with nature, surrounded by rainbows, waterfalls, beaches, and warm gentle rains. Most observed and worked with the ways of natural cycles, talking to them and giving thanks. Even the *pōhaku* (rocks) had their stories to tell if the listener was ready to hear them.

Most of these stories still heard today are gracious, revealing the intimate connection between all things and the deep love Hawaiians feel for their homelands. In Hawai'i one can almost smell the *mana* in the air. On the Big Island, healers also draw from the raw power of the volcanoes. The island is alive with the fire of creation, and new volcanic landmass is being continually created. This was and is a powerful force to use in all healing practices. Today it is common as well as culturally accepted throughout Polynesia to speak of various earth forces using goddesses (such as Pele or Poli'ahu) [11] on a daily basis, even on the evening news. Pele, who represents the powerful creation spirit of the volcanic activity of the islands, is captured below in an original painting by Mahealani Kuamo'o-Henry.

When this island lives in you, then you are truly living on the island. It speaks to you, often with gentle breezes that brush your cheek, and sometimes with a passionate rumble of change and upheaval. And once that happens, whether you stay or leave, you never will forget the feeling. It is what we call "paradise."

In addition to the healing arts, many events and occasions are done with ceremony, using *ti* leaves or Hawaiian salt, music, or chants and asking for the blessings and assistance of the *kūpuna* (elders or spiritual ancestors). An offering is called a *ho'okupu.* Traditionally, sweet potato, fruit, personal gifts, and treasures are wrapped and tied with *ti* leaves that have been "deboned" by removing the spine of the leaf. In more recent times, gifts to Pele, who "resides" in the Puna district of the Big Island, may include a small bottle of gin, said to be one of her favorite beverages. As you set down a gift, you feel the living volcanic earth under your feet. You feel humble, yet empowered. You know that you are not alone. At that moment you are overcome with awe at life itself and gratitude for all the blessings in your life. That is how it feels to truly pray, to do *pule*.

Papa Kepilino giving a hoʻokupu (offering) to Tūtū (grandmother) Pele at a steam vent in Hawaiʻi Volcanoes National Park.

No matter who you are or what your beliefs may be, you can pray. Do not ask for anything when you pray because that pushes the desired state out of the present moment. Instead, become mindful of the presence of spirit. There is truly nothing but spirit, manifested in an endless variety of densities and forms. Your job is to fine-tune yourself so that you can perceive and channel that which already is. From this place of remembering, you will be blessing your client as well as yourself. You can begin simply by holding a silent complimentary thought while praising a quality of your client. That begins the blessing—sending energy to another.

The Hawaiian language has a healing vibrational quality to it, engineered, it is said, by the ancients. Here is a nice prayer that can be used before or after a healing session:

Aloha e ke Akua. E ho'olohe i kā mākou pule ha'aha'a.
Mahalo a nui loa no kēia lā a me nā makana nui āu i hā'awi
maila. E ho'opōmaika'i mai iā mākou a pau me kou hau'oli,
ka maluhia a me ke aloha. 'Āmene.

(Greetings of love, O God. Listen to our humble prayer.
Thank you so much for this day and for the many gifts that
You have given us. Bless us all with Your joyfulness,
protection, and with Your Love. And so it is.)

Assessment

After *pule*, the session usually begins with a general assessment of the client's condition. Whatever the problem or condition may be, once identified, the focus shifts to and remains on the desired state. Visualize the highest possible outcome. *Lomi* should be done while the imagery of the perfect condition is held in intention. The proper modalities and remedies are chosen, but the energy shifts to the goal of the treatment, from the past or present to the future state. Then together all movement aims to bring that goal into the present moment.

The experienced practitioner tends to be familiar with most disorders and can recognize not only the symptoms but the underlying causes. The whole person is assessed, including physical structures, emotional tendencies, belief patterns, and the spiritual state. All aspects of self are addressed, either with words or touch. All sessions are body-mind oriented. Many Hawaiian healers can discern the underlying energetic causes of "dis-ease" in this manner, even over great distances. If others are involved, such as a problematic family member, they too will be included in the *pule.*

The truly spiritual methods of assessing disorders, as were commonly practiced in old Hawaiʻi, are very different from the analytical, objective process we see practiced in modern medicine. In both Western and Oriental orthodox medicine, a wide array of symptoms and diseases have been studied and categorized. The effects of subsequent medicines (pharmaceuticals and herbs) are also well researched and documented. Hawaiian methods, on the other hand, were practiced entirely on a grassroots level. There were no double-blind studies, textbooks, or research projects. Everything was based on testimonials, the wisdom of the elders, and the practitioner's skills and intuition. The client's belief system, his or her willingness to be healed, and faith in the various cures were and still are important to attain the desired results.

One of the greatest skills of the *kahuna lomilomi* was the ability to perform diagnostic palpation. The term for this is *hāhā,* which was defined in a 1922 dictionary as "to feel, as if searching for something." Palpating primarily the abdominal area, physical congestion, inflammation, and organ displacements were assessed. Many diagrams exist in manuscripts written in the years after European contact that depict dots in various arrangements within inverted triangles. In the region between the diaphragm and pubic bones, the various patterns represent different maladies and their corresponding symptoms. The Hawaiians would study the feel of these patterns by practicing the palpating of different arrangements of *'ili'ili* pebbles carefully laid out on a mat or piece of bark cloth on the ground (please see page 122). It is said that there were about 480 red, white, and black pebbles that were laid down in the shape of a man, and that 280 diseases could be identified. In this way the art of diagnosis was passed from *kahuna* to *haumāna* (student). The *haumāna* would perfect his or her touch by supervised practice on the sick. Perhaps this is one of the reasons Hawai'i, unlike other states, has always embraced the concept of an apprenticeship period in the training of massage therapists.

Drawings of various diseases for palpation purposes, 1876.

Another concept that was used in assessment is similar to, or may have been influenced by, the Oriental perception of external or internal influences on disease. *Ma waho* (external or outside cause) versus *ma loko* (internal or inside cause) would determine the proper course of treatment to remove the cause, thereby healing the problem. These concepts would include physical, emotional, and psychic causes of disease, and would often be revealed through visions or *moe'uhane* (dreams). During the *kapu* days, there existed a lot of *'anā'anā* (black magic) and deeply held beliefs and fears about offending one's superiors, such as the *ali'i*, *'aumākua*, *lapu* (disgruntled ghosts), and *kupua* (nature spirits).

Today's practitioners know that the art of assessment lies somewhere between the superstitions of the past and the rigid objectivity of modern science. "It's all in your mind" is no longer used to imply that something is not real or a separation of mind and body. Deep within all indigenous medicinal systems (based on the common welfare of the people, not just profit), we find common principles to restore health and prevent disease:

- Internal cleansing, particularly of the small and large intestines.
- Release or removal of obstructions, pathogens, damaging factors, and self-sabotaging beliefs.
- Positive attitude and proper thought.
- Sincere belief in, respect for, and acceptance of a higher power.
- Methods to improve circulation, such as sweat lodges and massage.
- Use of local substances to aid in healing, such as clay, plants, or herbs.
- Ceremonies for embracing major life transitions (birth, puberty, menopause, and death).
- Acceptance and faith in the traditional practices and in the practitioner who delivers the treatment.

Routine

There are many different *lomilomi* traditions from many different places on the islands. There is no absolute *lomilomi* routine. Each has its advantages and disadvantages. Some may encourage specific results, or stress certain body parts, but there are as many routines as there are *kūpuna* carrying on their unique lineage.

In the Bishop Museum archives are many references to *lomilomi* sessions beginning in a supine (lying on the back) position, working from the head down the front of the body and then up the back side starting at the feet. Other routines, on the other hand, begin prone (lying on the abdomen). Some offer elaborate analogies to correspond with different body parts and sequences. Beginners should start with the routine given by their *kumu*, modifying it as necessary or desirable as their personal experience and skill level develop. Seasoned therapists may use *lomilomi* as a substitute routine, or add certain *lomi* moves to their own.

The main purpose of any routine is to put the moves together in a flowing manner in an allotted amount of time, while covering most of the body with order and symmetry. Extra time and care should be given to areas requiring it, or if requested by the client. Often these areas include the neck and shoulders, between the shoulder blades, the low back, and legs. Other common sites include muscles frequently used in the client's occupation or sport, or areas compensating for postural and emotional imbalances.

Because *lomilomi* manipulates soft tissues using moderate to deep pressure, some areas may need to be avoided during a session. For a list of contraindications, see chapter 2. Please consult your *kumu*, a physician, or specialist if you are not trained in contraindications, as mechanical massage can damage or worsen certain conditions. If in doubt, don't. Above all: *Do no harm.* Instead, remember to always love the body!

In general, a full-body routine lasts from 60 to 90 minutes and should normally be done half face up (supine) and half face down (prone). Side-lying or seated positions are also used. In the past, a treatment could take hours or even days; today resorts often put 50-minute sessions on their menus.

Ideally, the whole body should be addressed, head to toe, excluding the genitalia and female breasts. Under the right circumstances, as in prenatal, midwifery, or lymphatic massage, these areas may be addressed. *Lomilomi* is not a sexual modality, nor should it at anytime make the client uncomfortable in this manner. Sexual massage is an entirely different subject from nurturing, therapeutic, and professional massage. When massaging your significant other, your only restrictions concern your partner's receptivity, comfort, and state of health. At all other times *all* sexual overtones are inappropriate, whether implied, contemplated, or enacted. It does not matter if you are working for compensation, donation, or giving away your services. Massaging another person is one of the most intimate, sacred things you can engage in and should never be done without complete mutual trust and respect. Some people are touch deprived or unable to differentiate between nurturing, healing, and sexual touch. Although the client or patient is usually unclothed, *lomilomi* is not a sexual initiation massage. It is a sacred, healing, holistic treatment with the utmost respect for the recipient, the practitioner, the practitioner's teachers, and God. The practitioner must always assume full responsibility for the content and outcome of the massage session because of the vulnerability of the client.

Practitioners often confuse results with skills. While every effort must be made to deliver the most effective and appropriate treatment, the practitioner must remember he or she is only a channel for the healing energies. Because some clients are not yet ready to let go of the past condition, nor fully able to receive the blessing of well-being and joy awaiting them, the practitioner may not achieve the results hoped for. Nevertheless, all sessions in real *lomilomi* end with a heartfelt *mahalo* (thank you) attitude.

Technique

This is where *lomilomi* shows its extreme diversity. Just as there is no absolute *lomilomi* routine, there is no one standard set of techniques. Some styles are done with the hands and feet (traditional *lomi* styles) and some also use the forearms (table styles). In every school it is taught a bit differently. It is considered respectful to do exactly what your *kumu* does in exactly the way he or she does it. In the old days, deviations were considered extremely disrespectful because they could leave the techniques vulnerable to being less sacred, less effective, or worse, lost to future generations. But today each practitioner does *lomi* in his or her unique way.

At first glance, *lomilomi* seems to be a Polynesian version of traditional European or Swedish massage. While the massage techniques are circulatory (moving body fluids like blood and lymph, as opposed to traditional Far Eastern techniques that primarily use pressure points to affect energy, nerves, and meridian flows), many practitioners teach that massage is only a small part of true *lomilomi*. Aupuni, a *kanaka maoli* teacher who heads the Kalama Foundation in the Pacific Northwest, compares *lomilomi* to the art of pulling *taro* and making *poi*. He teaches that it is a healing art that incorporates the physical, the mental, and the spiritual with the internal and external environments of the individual. To most native Hawaiians, *lomilomi* without the accompanying spiritual work is like swimming without water.

Most definitions of massage include some sort of manual manipulation of the soft tissues of the body. *Lomilomi* and classical European massage techniques glide and knead these soft tissues, which encompass the skin, muscles, and connective tissue surrounding them. To ease these techniques, oil or lubrication must be applied to the skin. Some of the floor *lomilomi* techniques resemble barefoot shiatsu, which does not require oil for the rocking and compression movements. *Lomilomi* today is usually done on a massage table, and relies on the application of oils (coconut, *kukui*, or vegetable) and hot stones, herbs, or salt water. While the whole person is loved unconditionally, muscles and connective tissue are stretched in length and width, stiff joints are loosened, circulation is improved, and internal organs are gently manipulated into their correct relationships. *Lomilomi* practitioners have a reputation for possessing exceptional palpation skills, listening to what the body is saying throughout the session with their hands and hearts.

The *kānaka maoli* are a strong race, usually equipped with effortless grace, large dense bones, smooth golden skin, a relaxed demeanor, and spontaneous laughter. They tend to be full-figured or athletic and very loving with deep, dark, empathetic eyes. They freely express emotions and are naturally sensual. They love to embrace, greeting friends and new acquaintances with a kiss on the cheeks rather than a handshake. This is not a traditional moist kiss, but rather a warm exchange of breath, or, in the old style, an exchange of breath from the nose with foreheads touching. Most Hawaiians have large hands and the most wonderful, fleshy forearms. Consequently, they make great therapists. They can work with ease with any part of their well-padded arms or hands, as their touch feels sincere, well cushioned, and nonintrusive.

Some Hawaiians do deep *lomilomi* primarily with the fingers and heels of the hands. Their hands "listen and talk" to each client's body, then move deep into the problematic tissues. They are masters at palpation and locating the bony structures as they "clean" or "wash the bone" with deep, slow strokes. Their fingers move in multidirectional strokes to disperse scar tissue and "knots" of tension in the muscles. Joints are stretched and occasionally adjusted. The body is lovingly but emphatically turned into pliable mush.

Many practitioners continue to work closely with the earth, using herbs, poultices, salt water, *ti* leaves, herbal salves from the *noni* plant, *lomi* sticks made from guava tree branches, warm lava rocks, and other tools to improve circulation, reduce swelling, numb pain, and realign the body.

The most widely practiced traditional-style techniques are found in the routine of Aunty Margaret Machado. She has probably had more students over the years than any other living *kupuna*, and is one of the few who are actually state licensed to practice and teach for compensation, as well as being of Hawaiian ancestry. Some people equate *lomilomi* with her routine, which includes a lot of forearm strokes and a 1-2-3 rhythm. Her *pule* are always Christian prayers, and she wisely stresses the importance of internal cleansing. She has many followers (both locals and foreigners) who are now teaching massage.

The other most widely used traditional style comes from Maui's late Kalua Kaiahua. Like Aunty Margaret, he taught way before massage became as popular and widespread as it is now. Such original teachers, many of whom are no longer with us, stepped forward to share their teachings when it was still *kapu* to do so, and they took some criticism from their peers for being a step ahead of the times.

Another very popular type of bodywork is the temple style, which is believed to be an interpretive blend of *lua* martial arts, *hula*, and massage from Kaua'i. This school of thought, like the Huna teachings, is very popular in Germany, Australia, and New Zealand. Some teachers of this style theorize that the moves originally came from ancient Egypt, and that the body was levitated during the session while the practitioner danced around it. Today these teachings use principles of Western New Age psychology and ancient African shamanism to facilitate a trance-like euphoric experience for exorbitant fees. While most of this work can be beneficial in its own right, and the healing principles are universal, it is not considered by the *kānaka maoli* to be native Hawaiian in origin. This upsets many Hawaiians, who feel their sacred ways are constantly exploited for profit.

Much of the general public is truly confused about what Hawaiian massage is. What makes *lomilomi* authentic? This is not an easy question to answer. The Hawaiians tend to stress that the gift or blessing be personally passed on from *kumu* to *haumāna*, and that the work be done for free as much as possible. Students who become practitioners in authentic *lomi* tend to be humble, learning or well-versed in the Hawaiian language and culture, skilled at *pule*, and always willing to give *aloha*—genuine, unconditional love and recognition of the living spirit within another—to others. The best practitioners, and especially the new generation of teachers, have been studying and practicing for many years with more than a few *kumu*, at least some of whom are native Hawaiian or Polynesian. In this way, the practitioners can take the very best from all styles and incorporate it into their own unique *lomilomi* session.

Massage Strokes

The following techniques are presented for reference and have been gathered from many oral and written sources. Teachers may or may not use these terms in their teachings. They may use others not listed here, or no terms at all. The presentation of these techniques is not meant to replace the personal training and guidance of a *kumu* or a class in *lomilomi*, so please seek professional training if you haven't already done so.

It is very important to gauge your pressure to the recipient's tolerance level. When doing deep work, take care that it "hurts soooo good" and then follow immediately with soothing strokes. Never inflict sudden, abrupt pain or damage tissue in the course of the session. Remember to use the breath[12] as you work. These massage techniques are primarily done with the forearm, palm of the hand, and fingers:

- **Lomilomi** (to rub, squeeze, crush, or knead). This term can be used for the kneading movements or for the massage treatment as a whole to describe the physical, mental, and spiritual healing process. The tissue is moved in every direction possible. The practitioner works gently but firmly to spread or break up tissues, similar to shredding apart the muscle fibers in a big piece of cooked meat. One should work with the fibers, separating them from one another. Or as Aunty Margaret often commented, "*lomilomi* resembles the alternate pawing of the claws of a contented cat."

  In the 1934 *Outline of Hawaiian Physical Therapeutics*, *lomi* is defined as "to knead, rub, or soothe" while "in its reduplicated intensive form, *lomilomi* signifies 'massage'." This term is also commonly used to describe a popular local dish consisting of diced salmon, tomatoes, and onions, similar to salsa, called "*lomilomi* salmon."

- **Kūpele** (to knead). Another term for kneading, this could be likened to *petrissage*, as it is done with an alternate kneading rhythm, using alternate circular movements to first compress then squeeze the soft "fleshy" tissues. Classical European styles are performed with the hands facing each other. *Lomi* styles are similar, with alternate overlapping circular movements, but the positions of the hands face the same direction, as shown above. This term is also used in Hawai'i to describe kneading hard fresh *poi.*

- **Kaomi** (to press down, pushing with downward pressure). This would describe any type of compression movement. The Hawaiians use their feet, forearms, fingers, and palms to compress the client's muscles. If you are patient, the tissue will "let you in" as it relaxes. In the Hawaiian language, this term is also used when describing suppressed thoughts.

- **Kahi** (to stroke or touch lightly). This would include light gliding strokes, or *effleurage*, as if gently stroking the back of a cat. It is extremely comforting. Sometimes it can be done with a good deal of pressure; other times it can refer to "therapeutic touch" without movement. *Kahi* can also be done perpendicular to the bones and muscle fibers.

   Although it is sometimes done in a downward or outward direction (toward the hands or feet), care should be given to do most gliding strokes upward on the arms and legs. This helps venous blood and lymphatic fluids to return to the heart, which is essential for inactive or bedridden patients, or in cases of edema, swelling, obesity, and kidney disease.

- **Kuʻi** (to pound, strike, beat out). This is called "percussion," or in French *tapotement*. The palms or fists rhythmically tenderize the thick tissues. Never perform this on bones or over damaged or delicate areas. This term is often used in *poi* preparation. For example, *pōhaku kuʻi ʻai* refers to a stone *poi* pounder that effectively smashes up the root of the *taro* into a paste. Thick *poi* (called "one-finger," which is dipped into the bowl to scoop out a mouthful) has less water mixed in it than does thin *poi* ("two-finger").

- **Hamo** (to anoint; to caress or rub with oil). This term could describe a blessing by a priest or *kahuna* because a substance is applied to the skin with spiritual intention. For this reason, I recommend using quality massage oils and well-focused intentions during this stroke. In *lomilomi* it is used for the first oiling strokes of each area, and various other rubbing and gliding movements.

- **'Ōpā** (to press and squeeze). Similar to "fulling" in Swedish massage, the hands compress and pull the muscles in a manner similar to kneading dough. As with all kneading movements, the tissues are softened and spread as the circulation is greatly enhanced.

Complementary Practices

As I emphasized earlier in the book, *lomilomi* is much more than massage. Practitioners make use of a wide variety of healing practices—including Hawaiian herbal medicines, which I touch on here but discuss in more detail in chapter 6. The following are complementary practices to the actual massage strokes of the *lomilomi* practitioners of yesterday and today:

- **Pī kai** (to sprinkle with salted water or seawater). This is done in blessings to remove any bad energy or lift *kapu* (taboo). It is a very popular ritual done during the opening of new businesses, completion of homes, and celebrations such as baptisms and marriages. It is similar to the Christian practice, except with the addition of salt. In Hawai'i a *tī* leaf is used rather than the hands.

- **Inu kai** (to drink salted water or seawater). After proper preparation and emptying of the bowels, a drink of salted water (see recipe, page 113) is taken on an empty stomach after days of eating high-fiber foods like fruits and sweet potatoes to thoroughly flush out the small and large intestines. The Hawaiians used clean local seawater, diluting it to one part seawater to two parts freshwater. This is practiced  frequently by most *lomilomi* teachers on Hawai'i island who stress the importance of internal cleansing.

- **Hihi wai** (to intertwine water with oil). After applying massage oil to the back, a second application of warm water from a bowl with a little Hawaiian salt mixed in it can be added. This is for purification and to keep the oil on the skin from getting tacky. In cold climates, make sure to re-drape the wet area once the water has cooled to keep your client warm. *Hihi* means "to intertwine," and *wai* refers to water or any fluid other than *kai* (salt water).

- **Hō'upu'upu** (thought implantation or suggestion). Similar to an affirmation, the spoken word, or *'ōlelo*, was known to precede all form. During *lomilomi*, *hō'upu'upu* for practitioner and patient would help manifest the desired state of health on all levels. *'Upu* means "a recurring thought or hope." This would often begin before and continue after the treatment.

- **Pōhaku wela and lā'au lomi** (to use hot rocks and *lomi* sticks). Some of the common tools the Hawaiians use include stones that have been heated in the fire pit and *lomi* sticks made from guava branches. The hot stones can be loosely wrapped with a *ti* or *noni* leaf, then placed on the problem areas of the client. Or, once cooled sufficiently, they can be used as an extension of the hands to massage the tissue directly. Today stones can be conveniently heated in roasters, crock pots, or microwave ovens.

Remember, if they are too hot to hold, they are too hot for direct application on your client's skin. Use stones to warm your hands first, and apply to the client once it is safe. Below (left) shows an ideal way to heat your stones.

Guava branches are selected for their perfect "7" angle (about 45 degrees), as shown in photo above on right. One branch is left longer than the other, then they are crafted down to a smooth shape and flattened tip until the stick comfortably wraps around the body. Then they are pressed into the tight muscular areas.

- **Lāʻau lapaʻau** (herbal medicine). The *kahuna lāʻau lapaʻau* (herbal master or priest) or *kauka lāʻau lapaʻau* (doctor of herbal medicine) heals the patient with traditional herbal treatments, internally and externally. Today there are many nurseries, classes, and books about Hawaiian herbal medicines. Below a hot stone is used over a *ti* leaf on the client's back.

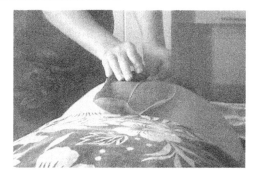

- **Hālalo poʻi** (poultice or decoction of herbs). It was common to apply mashed up mixtures of herbs like *ʻawa* root, *mamaki, noni,* morning glory, *honohono* grass, gota kola, or aloe vera for relief of muscular pain, sprains, abrasions, fractures, toothaches, boils, and insect bites, to name a few. Like many herbs, Hawaiian plants have astringent, germicidal, anti-inflammatory, and analgesic properties. **Hālalo poʻi** means "to make deep or go downward; with a cover."

- **Hāhā** (to feel or palpate). The art of feeling tissue with the fingertips is an essential assessment tool for all massage therapists, and the Hawaiians excelled at it. Diagnoses are made by *lomilomi* practitioners and doctors to detect inflammation, congestion, scar tissue, misplacements, blockages, and dislocations. *Kāhuna* could "see with their hands" with amazing accuracy.

- **Hāhā i ka ʻōpū huli** (to treat "turned stomach" and indigestion). This method of deep *hoʻohuli ʻōpū* work massages down the descending colon on the left and up the ascending colon on the right, adding vibrations up the sides of the waist. This brings relief to gastrointestinal disturbances. This is a widespread practice in Hawaiʻi and clears the small and large intestines, enabling the contents of the stomach and digestive tract to move freely. The *naʻau* (source of instincts) is located in the *ʻōpū*, and this center is more valued for guidance by the Hawaiians than is the *manaʻo* (intellect). It is important not to skip this part of the body.

- **Pūloʻuloʻu** (steam bath). This old form of physical therapy, as described by historian David Malo, was done in a *hale hau* (little hut made of arched *hau* branches). Heat came from stones that were heated in a fire pit covered with leaves and herbs, similar to a native American sweat lodge. Makaʻala Yates, pictured below, regularly builds *hale pūloʻuloʻu* at his workshops, using Hawaiian chants and herbs as part of the purification process. Be sure to drink a lot of pure water before, during, and after a sweat.

- **Lāʻau kāhea** (calling forth the healing). This is a rare practice of breathing *mana* into an ill person or affected area to restore life or heal bones. Because bone is living tissue, the *hā*, or sacred breath, of the *kahuna* could energize even fractures. A few could cause a perceptible "wave" of healing *mana* to penetrate deep into the tissues while chanting a *pule* as they would breathe over the affected site. The *lāʻau kāhea* might also be used to "call" life back into a drowning victim, for example.

- **Hoʻoponopono** (forgiveness; realignment). This body-mind technique is so important, I have devoted the following section to it. Widely practiced in various forms today, it has always been key to ridding a person of self-defeating and disease-causing ill feelings, limited beliefs, lingering resentments, stubborn grudges, and pent-up anger.

Ho'oponopono

Rid yourself of all regrets about the past.
Guilt is a useless emotion.
It doesn't do any good for anyone.

—Ancient Hawaiian teaching of *ho'oponopono*

My favorite Hawaiian word is *pono,* meaning excellence, righteous, moral, prosperous, successful, proper, just, fair, and necessary. Literally translated, *ho'opono* means "to bring into action the state of being *pono."* By repeating the word *pono* twice it can imply to correct something that is definitely not *pono.* When we correct the wrongs—wrong thoughts, feelings, attitudes, and beliefs—it functions as a body-mind-spirit balancer.

This practice was and still is used to correct or clear the air in important situations where harmony is severely absent. Today it is defined in many ways, including forgiveness, conflict resolution, mental cleansing, self realignment, and "to put things right." It is often used in counseling, or between family or group members or to get things "off one's chest." In this way, resentments and misunderstandings are not left to fester, causing further confusion or "dis-ease."

Lomilomi cannot provide long-term benefits without addressing the mental and emotional condition of the individual. Today the physiological effects of stress are well documented, and the relationship between unresolved emotions and negative beliefs are well understood. The Hawaiians knew that holding on to resentment, guilt, and similar emotions tended to fester within and lead to greater problems. *Ho'oponopono* is a powerful method to clear up misunderstandings, ideally before the sun sets each day. Everyone takes turns speaking his or her piece, forgiving one another, and, in this way, the family unit and community continue to function in harmony. Healing and harmony, in any language, ultimately require total and complete forgiveness of self and others.

In her book *Ho'opono*, historian Aunty Pali Jae Lee states, "If it is good, if it is in balance, if it is right, if it helps, if it is righteous, if it is responsible, if it is caring, if it honors, if it is humble, if it is peaceful, if it is neat, if it is correct, if it is proper, and if it is well-mannered, it is *pono.*" She explains that being *pono* was what every person in old Hawai'i would strive to be, and if they got off track, the family elders would firmly but lovingly steer them back on course. If an individual chose to continue not to live in *pono*, harming himself and others, he would eventually be cast out of the family, which was the ultimate dishonor.

According to Kauka (doctor) Maka'ala Yates, *ho'oponopono* is considered by Hawaiians to be a sacred and effective approach to creating peace, love, health, and happiness in one's daily life. This ancient Hawaiian process, if integrated for today's use, allows for the release of problems and blocks that may cause stress, imbalance, and disease within oneself. "It is about creating true freedom and eliminating old fears, emotions, ideas and reactions," he teaches, "which contribute to psychological distresses and physical illnesses. [It can] assist in eliminating the conditioning that has polluted our existence for so long—much the way we erase useless information stored in a computer."

Another outstanding line of teachings comes from the late Mornea Simeona. She is pictured here (fourth from right) at a 1986 conference at the 'Ohana Keauhou Beach Hotel in Keauhou, Kona, with her assistant Stan, the crew members of the *Hōkūle'a* voyaging canoe, and the Roy family.

A *kumu* who was in many ways years before her time, she took these concepts of clearing, forgiving, and self-responsibility to the next level. She taught about karma and reincarnation. Years before she passed to the spirit level, she traveled the world, teaching and encountering souls with whom she felt deep *aka* (invisible, shadowy, energetic) connections. Her intention was to sever and resolve all of her karmic connections, clearing the way to the final graduation from the density of the earth-plane existence.

According to Mahealani Kuamo'o-Henry, each one of us has the responsibility to make more "mindful" choices everyday of our lives. She states, "*Pono* begins in thoughts that create well-being in one's mental and physical experiences through daily living." She teaches that if we mindfully choose to live *pono* in every situation and moment, we will experience "at-one-ness" with Akua—life as it was meant to be. By separating the words, her definition of *ho'opono pono* becomes "making what is right, more right." This allows us to start from the premise that each individual is born spiritually perfect as the ancient Hawaiians believed before the missionaries arrived, rather than in sin.

In this work, certain principles are accepted:

- Our ancestors or spirit guides are always with us, willing to assist us if only we ask. Although they have passed from physical to spiritual reality, they can communicate to us through our thoughts.
- The universe is spiritual, eternal, and infinite in essence. Spirit greatness is thus everybody's true identity and source, always and forever.
- Each individual has free will. With the help of the ancestors and knowing our true identity, each of us can choose to live moment-to-moment in the greatness and wisdom of spirit or in the darkness and confusion of being disconnected from it.
- Each individual is solely responsible for his or her choices, which ultimately affects all aspects of his or her life's experiences. There are no accidents.
- The greatest personal power an individual can attain is in living in the present moment, aligned by choice with the indwelling presence of God.

Nā kūpuna teach that everyone is born "a perfect bowl of light" and that as experiences accumulate in one's life, "dark stones" tend to fill this bowl, blocking out the light. It is each individual's responsibility to consciously *hoʻohuli* (turn over) their bowls, releasing the hurts and dark energies and allowing the *aloha* and light of spirit greatness to shine once again. Then one must walk the talk and live mindfully.

The powerful forces of love and fear bring *pono* or *pilikia* (troubles), which can lighten or burden the heart, creating conditions that affect the rest of the body, as we all have experienced. While the *mana'o* (intellect) serves us diligently, creating and processing our thoughts, it tends to try to overpower the more subtle thoughts and intuitions from our spirit. "It tends to get carried away with itself," laughs Mahealani. "The *pu'uwai mele* (singing heart or heart song) can also lead us astray if not balanced with the *mana'o* and, most important, the *na'au.* Living in *pono* enables us to avoid repeating patterns of excessive trauma and drama."

Abbie Napeahi, Eleanor Ahuna, and Mona Kahele are also well known on the Big Island for their dedicated *ho'oponopono* work in the community. For many years they've skillfully counseled people by taking them step-by-step through a resolution process that starts with *pule,* then discussion to unravel and untangle the issues "like the layers of an onion" before resolution and closing. Once the problems, upsets, and misunderstandings have been clearly identified and prioritized, it is essential to *kala* (release) and *'oki* (sever) the "knots" or pains. After a closing process and prayer, a much-welcomed happiness returns.

E lawe i ke aʻo a mālama,
a e ʻoi mau ka naʻauao.

Take what is learned and care for it,

and knowledge will always be increased.

❦ 5 ❦

Hands-on

Before You Begin

Before beginning a massage, you should prepare yourself and the space in which the session will take place. Take a moment to be still and disengage from your personal affairs. Ask for divine assistance. Ask that whatever needs to be restored, be restored; and whatever needs to be released, released. Know that there is always a larger picture beyond your comprehension, and do not be attached to your preconceived notions of how the healing process should unfold.

Each person is going through a unique journey on this planet, and, on some level, each of us creates our own path. Even if this concept is difficult for you to comprehend, know that it is truly each person's responsibility to heal and receive the benefits of the *lomilomi* treatment deeply into his or her being. The therapist has the sacred task of being the best facilitator he or she can be, and the quality of the treatment directly reflects the state of being achieved and lived day to day by the therapist.

The same rules in all massage styles apply to *lomilomi:* Wash your hands before and after every session, give your patients your full and uninterrupted attention, make them comfortable, and do an assessment first. Why have they come to you? What injuries or surgeries, if any, have they incurred? Where are the areas of compensatory tension? What do they really need from you? What is their emotional state of health? Can you keep a professional distance from your clients? Can you visualize their perfect beings in perfect states of health, and hold that vision? Can you maintain unconditional *aloha*?

Today we drape our clients for modesty and warmth, undraping each part of the body as we massage it. The art of draping takes time to master, but when done well, it can allow clients to safely drift away, beyond concerns of their physical "flaws" or inappropriate touching. Hawaiians would usually wear minimal clothing, like a *malo.* Nude massage is not practiced except on babies and toddlers. Professional massage keeps the sacred and private areas of the body covered; sexual massage between partners is another matter. When working on your sweetheart, draping is optional.

Indications and contraindications are the same as with other types of deep tissue bodywork, so make sure you have had the proper training before attempting to be a massage therapist. Again, this reference book is not intended to serve as a training manual.

To achieve maximum results and experience the rewards of applying therapeutic touch, learn to charge up your personal supply of *mana* before you start. And after each session, remember to release all your energetic ties as you bless the client and say good-bye.

The following pages show some of my favorite *lomilomi* moves in a full-body routine as demonstrated by Paul Rambo, LMT, former administrative assistant and primary instructor at my Hilo massage school during the 1990s. This particular routine is a mixture of techniques from many of the teachers discussed in this book. Every *kumu* has different techniques and a unique way of presenting them. Some practitioners use these Hawaiian terms, and some do not. Some terms have been coined in the last few decades. Some practitioners emphasize rhythm, some cleansing, some specific sequences, and some focus on certain parts of the body. Each has his or her own routine. Many work from the foot to the head instead of head to foot. There are many approaches, and that is fine as long as it is done in a way that is *pono*.

The important thing is how effectively, thoroughly, and lovingly the therapist massages the soft tissues of the body. Approach each section with reverence, and establish trust with your touch. Remember to first warm up the tissue, then work deeply, and always finish with soothing strokes on every major body part. Never be intrusive. Keep the client draped for warmth and modesty. Work from general to specific, light to deep pressure. Check periodically to see how your client is doing, especially after deep work.

In order to learn *lomilomi* correctly, it is important that you study with a teacher whom you respect. Then find other teachers, and study with them as well. There are several exceptional teachers on the islands whom you will find once you begin to look. There are also many good teachers in the US mainland, Europe, and elsewhere. A good rule of thumb is to shop around and ask prospective teachers questions to determine the quality of their work. Who were their teachers, and do they honor them? Are their fees overpriced? Do they live *aloha* unconditionally? Do they claim their teachings are "secrets," or do they openly share with those who have a sincere heart? Do they brag about their knowledge, or give themselves titles? Do they honor other practitioners? Do they know their anatomy? Do they put God first? Seek out several teachers, and, above all, use discernment.

Giving a therapeutic massage takes training and practice to assure that you do not injure your client or your own body. *Lomilomi* can easily be combined with other modalities or worked into your existing routine. Keep practicing! A good massage is one of the nicest things you can do for another person. Remember to keep practicing your *ho'oponopono*. And never stop learning.

Summary of Massage Terms in Routine

hamo:	applying oil with spiritual intention
kahi:	therapeutic touch; gliding strokes
kaomi:	compression movements
kīko'oko'o:	stretching movements
kūpele:	alternate kneading with hands
lomilomi:	soothing kneading movements
'ōpā:	squeezing and spreading movements
pule:	prayer
ulna *lomi*:	alternate forearm kneading
ulna push:	forearm gliding while lunging
wiggley-wiggley:	back and forth rocking movement up the spine

Prone Techniques *(face down)*

1. *Hamo* and *kahi*. Standing at the head of the table, apply oil with long, slow gliding strokes on the entire back. Beginning at the lower neck, slowly glide both of your palms all the way down the back and back up the sides. Repeat several times, each time reaching farther down toward the small of the back, past the lower rib cage. You should lean into your work, dropping your weight into your palms and/or thumbs while keeping your elbows straight, getting deeper each time on the muscles next to the spinal column. As you return up the sides of the back, contour your hands to match the shape of the body. This is like a classic "basic stroke."

Remember that *hamo* is a blessing as well as the initial application of oil. Focus your intention on your client as you encourage him or her to relax and breathe.

Never put deep pressure on the "floating" ribs just above the waist. There are many layers of muscles running right next to the vertebral column that need deep pressure on most people, but never press on the spine itself. This is an excellent time to assess tension in the back muscles through palpation.

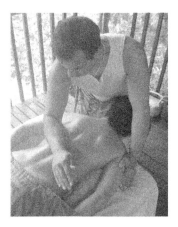

2. Ulna push. While shifting your weight from side to side, your left and right forearms take turns gliding down each side of the client's back and upper arms, taking care not to hit the spinous processes of the vertebral column. Use your hand and forearm as one unit. Step forward with your left foot at the same time as you massage with your left arm, and vice versa. Follow the contours of the back, from shoulder down to waist or elbow, with medium pressure. For best results, keep your forearm prone (palm down). Return with the palm of your hand. (The ulna is the bone from your elbow to your wrist in line with your little finger.)

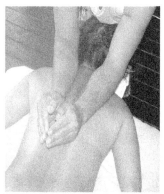

3. Double wiggley. Using the blades of both hands, gently glide down the back with a sideways rocking motion.

4. Ulna *lomi*. Step to the side of your client. Oil your forearms and position them so that the "ulna flesh" of your prone forearm rests on the fleshy part of the back, not the bones of the spinal column. Make big overlapping, alternate circles on the back in a steady rhythm. The left arm moves counterclockwise, followed by the right arm moving clockwise. Keep your pressure light to medium, especially over the kidneys and floating ribs (pairs 11 and 12) of the lower rib cage.

While standing with legs several feet apart and knees bent, keep shifting your weight from left to right. Vary the degree of bend in your elbow so that you can cover all the muscles on the side of the back nearest you, including the ones on the shoulder blade. Go lightly on protruding bones such as the edges of the shoulder blades. This is a *lomi* kneading move with a multidirectional effect on the tissues.

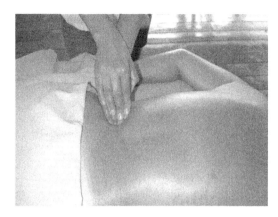

5. Low back. With reinforced (hand-on-hand) fingertips, lean with your body weight into your braced hands and slowly probe into the thick connective tissue of the back and sacrum. Approach at an oblique angle a few inches from the vertebrae, and go slowly enough so that the tissue releases under your pressure as it softens and relaxes sufficiently. Then make deep circles into the quadratus lumborum muscle next to the lumbar spine, releasing deep postural tension.

Take care to keep your elbow, wrist, and finger joints straight. You are just above the pelvis, but below the ribs. Increase your pressure gradually to the client's tolerance. Then soothe with a few **wiggley-wiggley** strokes, dragging your fingers in a zig-zag manner up the spine, as shown below.

6. *Poʻohiwi* (shoulder) push/pull. Gently scoop one hand under the shoulder joint to support it while the other hand is free to massage the rhomboids, probing for tight areas. Using a slow, deep stroke, glide up and down the muscles between the shoulder blade and spinal column with the blade of your hand and your forearm. Drop your weight in a downward direction into your client's back muscles, avoiding the spine. Ask for feedback on your pressure for possible pain. Then soothe while your hands move in opposite directions—one upward while the other moves downward, and vice versa.

Most people have layers of tension in the shoulders and neck. Take time to thoroughly massage the many muscles between and above the shoulder blades, one side at a time. Use your forearm near your elbow, which is bent at a 90 degree angle (rather than the pointed tip of the elbow).

In this position, some practitioners like to place the client's arm behind (on) the low back. This makes the inner scapula more accessible as it pops out. But it also medially rotates the joint to its limit, which can be uncomfortable. The shoulder should not be kept in this position for long. If the client has a prior injury to the shoulder, leave the arm on the table.

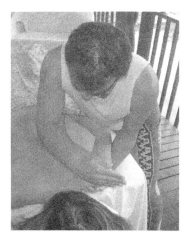

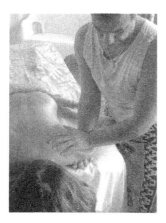
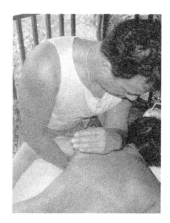

7. Circling. Make sure the client's arm is lying flat on the table for both of these strokes. Now we are going to switch hands. Lift the shoulder and carefully slide your other hand, palm up, under the joint and armpit. It will be resting between the client's body and arm. Place your other palm face down on top of the joint, as shown below. With one hand above and one below the shoulder, palms facing each other, make reciprocating circles in a staggered manner. Continue first clockwise with both hands, then counterclockwise with both hands. You should feel the weight of the shoulder in your bottom hand, which is relaxed and making smaller circles than your top hand. The shoulder blade should move freely under your top hand.

This loosens the shoulder blade and upper back muscles. For deeper work, use your forearm on top of the shoulder placed parallel and next to the spine, and lean into the muscles between the scapula and vertebrae, as shown. Check that the pressure is within your client's tolerance, and make sure you are between (not on) the scapula and vertebral column. Also keep your bottom palm relaxed. If you bend your elbow, you can wrap around the top of the scapula, massaging the levator scapula and upper trapezius muscles.

8. *Lomi* and *'ōpā*. While supporting the elbow, move the arm so it hangs over the edge of the table. Knead the entire length of the arm in a rhythmic manner. Although you will work progressively down from the shoulder to the wrist, each overlapping stroke pushes in an upward direction. The pressure should be medium and is equally divided between your thumbs and pads of the fingers, grasping and compressing the tissues in an alternating kneading rhythm. Do not dig into the muscles with your fingertips; use the flat pads instead.

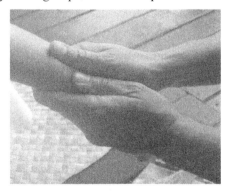

If using a mat or table with a face hole instead of a headrest, *lomi* the arm while it rests on the mat or table. Take care not to pinch the muscles and skin.

9. Deep *kahi.* Supporting under your client's elbow with your free hand (as shown below), lunge as you do a gliding stroke from the elbow to the scapula and then lightly back again. Use your palm and forearm, focusing on the infraspinatus, teres minor, and teres major muscles as shown. When the arm is in this upward abducted position, the shoulder blade is flat and easy to glide over. Then soothe with several long palm strokes from the elbow down to the waist. Follow through and return with your palm.

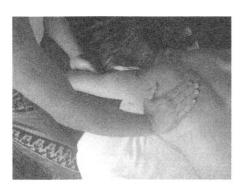 

When you are massaging with your right arm, you are lunging into your right leg, and vice versa, following the contours of the body with carefully directed pressure. Make sure to press firmly into the muscles on top of the shoulder blade; otherwise, the pressure is light to medium only. The focus here is on the teres minor and infraspinatus muscles. Ease your pressure as you continue down the back and rib cage.

Take care not to lift the client's elbow too high as this may hyperextend the shoulder joint. The client's elbow should remain lower (closer to the floor) than the shoulder and head.

10. Forearm *kaomi*. Place the arm back on the table, supporting it with your cupped palm underneath, as shown above. Leaning over your work, slowly apply pressure with your inside forearm (not your elbow) to the muscles of the client's forearm. Begin lightly, increase gradually, hold, and release slowly. Lean into it, using your body weight. Your forearm is parallel to the floor and perpendicular to the client's arm, and your fingers point away from the back. Slowly progress downward toward the hand, making sure to move your palm down so that it always supports the client's forearm under your pressure. Ease up on your pressure over the wrist and elbow joints.

To follow with soothing strokes, *hamo* back up and *lomilomi* down the entire arm, finishing with the palm. Using your thumbs, support then *kūpele* the palm of the hand.

11. Switch sides. Switch sides, and repeat the shoulder and arm strokes to the other side of the body, connecting back, shoulder, and arm in a series of fluid movements. Then massage the back of the neck, focusing on the suboccipital muscles below the head.

Before moving on to the legs, massage the back again if time permits. Focus on the areas of tension that needed more work. Since they are already relaxed and warmed up, this is an excellent time for deep work, hot stones, towels, and pain-relieving oils and liniments. The low back area almost always requires additional attention. Many people suffer from posture or disc problems, which tightens the muscles on either side of the lumbar spine, just above the pelvis. Massage with firm circles over the sacrum. The muscles of the buttocks also benefit from massage like ulna *lomi* and slow forearm *kaomi* and can make a nice transition into the leg sequences that follow. Always finish with light-to-medium soothing strokes, then cover the back to keep the client warm.

12. Leg *kahi* and *lomilomi.* Undrape one leg at a time from hip to foot, tucking your top sheet securely under the client's thigh. With long slow strokes, *hamo* the entire leg as you apply the oil. Then slowly and deeply glide up the thigh muscles several times with palms and forearm, as shown. You can also do some slow *kaomi* on the hamstrings, but avoid the back of the knee.

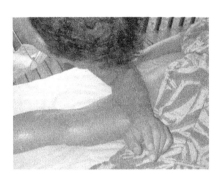
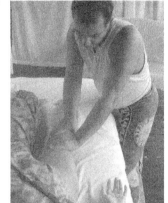

Then do *lomilomi* down the thigh to soothe. Although you are progressing down the leg, the strokes are pushing fluids upward.

Repeat the sequence on the lower leg with some firm upward gliding strokes with your palms up the calf, followed by soothing *lomilomi* down the calf to the foot. This is very good for circulation in the legs.

13. *Poi* pounder. Bend the knee, holding the ankle as shown below. Lift the leg straight up so that the thigh is just off the table, and then gently pound it back down three times. Now that the front of the thigh is warmed up by these compressions, slowly *kīko'oko'o* (stretch) the thigh by touching the heel to the buttocks.

Here is a good point to do range-of-motion on the leg and hip. Place the leg in the crook of your arm, as shown below. Place your other forearm on the gluteal muscles, and, in a deep lunge, make big circular movements with both arms. While working the left leg as shown, move counterclockwise. When doing the other side, both arms will move in a clockwise circle.

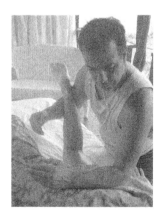

14. Calf ʻōpā. Now with the knee still bent, rest the client's foot on your shoulder as you sit on the edge of the table. Slowly glide down the calf muscles from the heel toward the knee, "milking" the calf as you stroke downward. Then with firm strokes, massage the sole of the foot as shown. The bottom of the foot likes deep pressure.

Place the leg back down, and do full-leg forearm gliding strokes toward the heart to flush the tissue fluids. Finish with deep forearm gliding strokes on the bottom of the foot while supporting under the ankle.

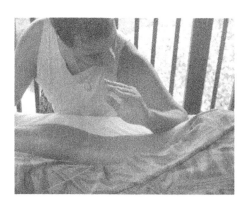

Re-drape and repeat the entire leg sequence on the other leg. Then *hoʻohuli* (turn over) your patient.

Supine Techniques *(face up)*

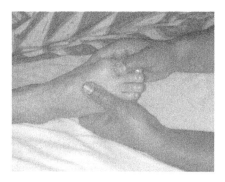

15. Foot massage. First make sure your client is comfortable, adjusting pillows or bolsters if needed. Massaging the feet is one of the most enjoyable and therapeutic moments in the massage because of the tens of thousands of sensory nerve endings. The dorsal (top, as shown above) side has many veins, so, with your thumbs, lightly stroke upward from the toes toward the ankle. Then with your thumbs or fists, deeply massage the bottom of the foot, as shown below.

This is a great time to use hot stones and work the toes and reflexology points. If the feet are dirty, use a hot towel to wipe them off first, or massage through the socks or top sheet.

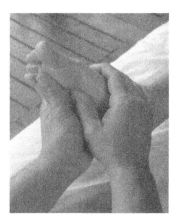
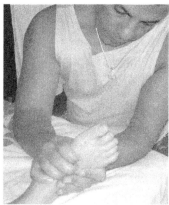

16. Leg *hamo* and ulna *lomi*. First undrape one leg, tucking the top sheet under the thigh. Then *hamo* the entire leg toward the heart, applying a generous amount of oil and positioning your hands to contour around the shin bone and kneecap, as shown above. Increase your pressure as you lean into the quadriceps and glide up the thigh, using your forearm if necessary. This is the strongest muscle group in the body.

Then do ulna *lomi* in big alternate, overlapping circles all over the thigh, as shown above. Do not ulna *lomi* directly over the groin or on the patella (kneecap).

17. *Lomilomi* and *kahi*. Soothe the thigh with full-palm *lomilomi,* progressing down the thigh gradually. Take care not to pinch or dig into the thigh with your fingers or thumbs.

Then move to the shin with alternate *kahi* gliding strokes, always working in an upward direction as you slowly increase your pressure. The tibialis anterior (just lateral to the tibia, or shin bone) loves deeper pressure, so use the heel of your hand or forearm with bent elbow (as shown below) to deeply and slowly glide up the muscle. Stop well before the patella, and make sure you are not pressing too deeply on the fibula.

Finish the front of the leg with long palmar *kahi* strokes upward, moving the fluids toward the heart and away from the ankles and feet as you lunge toward the head of the table. Then cover the leg and undrape the other one, tucking the top sheet and repeating the entire leg sequence on the other leg.

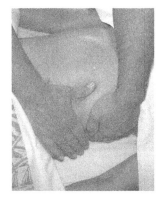

18. ***Hoʻohuli ʻōpū.*** Undrape the *ʻōpū* (abdomen) down to the ASIS (anterior, superior iliac spine) of the pelvis, leaving the breasts covered with a small towel or a pillowcase if your client is female. Make sure your hands are warm. Place both palms on the *ʻōpū.* Slowly *hamo* in three medium-pressure, counterclockwise circles. Then switch to clockwise for three more. Ask if your client would like deeper work in this area. If not, just finish with some energy work and more circles. If so, elevate or bend the knees to relax the rectus abdominis muscle. Then deeply but gently work the descending, transverse, and ascending colon. Continue with vibrations and soothing strokes within the client's comfort level. Re-drape when finished.

In Hawaiian healing, *ʻōpū huli* (turned abdomen) is a condition requiring deep cleansing of the gastrointestinal tract. The treatment consists of massage and herbal or saltwater internal colon cleansing (refer to chapter 7, Aunty Margaret). Make sure you receive proper training in this procedure before proceeding.

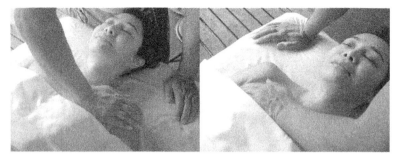

19. *Kahi.* Now we will massage the chest and arms. Begin with the pectoralis muscles. *Hamo* and *kahi* in a slow, outward direction with palms, the hands positioned as shown above. Then move to the side of the table. While supporting the elbow, lift it and apply oil in long strokes from the elbow, past the armpit, and along the side of the body. Keep your palm close to the table, as shown below on left.

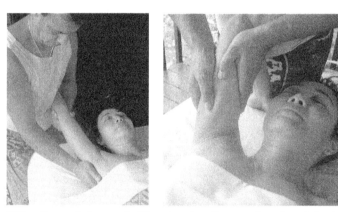

20. *Kūpele* and *kaomi.* Allowing the elbow to bend and the hand to rest on the head of the table, stabilize it with your body. Then *kūpele* the triceps with smooth overlapping strokes, using your full palms and not just your thumbs, as shown above on right.

Then return the arm to the client's side. Stand near the hand, facing the shoulder. After several deep *kahi* strokes up the forearm's brachioradialis muscle and medium strokes up the entire arm, *kaomi* down the forearm.

Then *lomilomi* down the entire arm from the shoulder to the wrist. Finish with the client's hand, kneading the palm and massaging the fingers. The palm can tolerate deep pressure. Make sure to *kahi* the veins on the top (dorsal side) of the hand toward the heart with light soothing strokes.

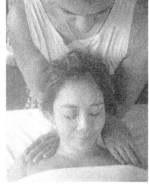

21. Neck stretches and *kūpele*. Warm up the neck muscles, working your fingers deeply into the back of the neck. Gently lift the head up off the table, using the leverage of your forearms. This stretches all the back and posterior neck muscles. Move slowly, never bouncing into the deep stretch positions or forcing the stretch. Take care not to strain your own back as you lift the head.

It is never too late to assess the client's condition, checking for pain, major surgeries, skin problems, or injuries. The joints of the body do not like extreme stretches if there is degeneration or recent trauma that has damaged the tissues. Many people suffer from old whiplash injuries, so be aware of any overprotectiveness on the part of your client.

Then lay the head down, and continue massaging the back of the neck and the upper trapezius muscles with *kūpele* strokes. This supine position is an effective way to utilize the weight of the client's head to access the deeper tissues.

22. Po'o. Massage on the *po'o* (head) helps calm the thoughts. If desired, your routine can begin here (supine first). Massaging in circles all over the scalp with firm pressure can be extremely effective.

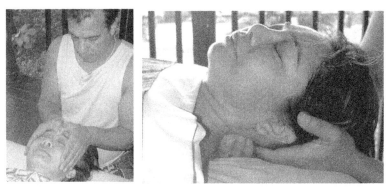

A complete massage on the face can be done at this point. You can excuse yourself to wash your hands. A hot facecloth can be used to wipe away excess dirt and oil while opening the pores of the skin. A light cream or oil (like avocado or *kukui* nut) should be used on the face. The earlobes are also good places to massage. Gently roll and stretch them between your thumbs and index fingers. Except for the eyes, nose, mouth, and throat areas, firm, medium pressure is usually appropriate. While standing over your client, take care not to talk or exhale in his or her face.

23. Closing *pule*. Take a deep breath, ask to be filled with unconditional love, and say a prayer of your choice, either aloud or silently.

Now is the time to begin to release yourself from the intimacy of your session. Always remember that everyone is fully responsible for his or her own well-being. Remember that you are a channel for God's healing energy. Visualize the perfect state of health of your client. Both of you should take a deep breath of gratitude. Breathe in *mana;* breathe out *aloha.* Bless your client and give thanks. *Mahalo, pau! 'Āmene.* (Thank you, it is finished. Amen. And so it is.)

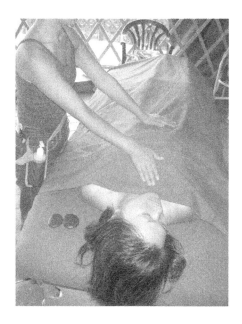

I pa`a ke kino o ke keiki i ka lā`au.

That the body of the child

be solidly built by the medicines.

⚘ 6 ⚘

Hawaiian Medicines

Lāʻau Lapaʻau

The use of traditional medicines is one of the bodies of knowledge in the Hawaiian culture that has endured. Although the knowledge of the traditional use of plant medicines is plentiful, the actual daily practice is not widespread, as Hawaiʻi imports more than 80 percent of its foods and medicines from the US mainland.

Herbal *lāʻau* (medicines) have direct physiological effects on the body. Medicinal trees, bushes, fruits, and flowers grow wild throughout the islands and are often valued for their ornamental beauty. Twelve months of the year, one can find an array of healing herbs and weeds to gather from the mountains to the coast. Using them properly as medicines, however, is an art and a science. Unsupervised experimentation and a partial understanding of the usage of botanicals can lead to illness or death. Many plants used in Hawaiian healing are today classified as toxic.

The *kahuna lāʻau lapaʻau* (herbal medicine expert) mastered the art of formulating compounds and prescribing remedies. In ancient times, much was known about botanical medicines. Recipes were passed down within the *ʻohana,* and villagers knew who specialized in different areas of treatment.

The numbers four and five predominated in medicinal practices, and elders today still refer to these numbers when counting or measuring something by the "handful." Gathering, which was usually done in the early morning with great reverence and concentration, was part of the elaborate healing ceremony. Days of precise methods of preparation and consumption of the prescribed herbs and foods were carefully executed, often in multiples of five. For example, a quantity of very young guava leaves might be plucked and consumed in bunches of five for diarrhea, or plants might be eaten for "five times five" days in succession for more chronic ailments. Counting fish or *taro* by *kauna* (fours) is an old custom found among most Pacific islanders.

Illustrations found in old medical writings depict the upper trunk of the body from *piko* (navel) to *umauma* (chest). These charts were drawn to represent the patterns and areas of illness felt through palpation skills. *Hāhā* (diagnosis by skillful feeling of tissues) was well developed in Hawaiʻi. Bumps or firm areas found alone or in rows or masses gave specific information as to the nature of the disease. These *hāhā* charts were also used in the instruction of the *haumāna* (student), who would practice palpation on *papa ʻiliʻili* (a table of pebbles). Layouts of small stones were used to represent the body, or, in the instruction of astronomy, the night sky. Please see page 122 for an illustration.

Once an illness was diagnosed, the prescriptions were made. Much of the medicinal knowledge was revealed to the *kahuna* by the *'aumākua* in dreams. As with all medicines, the correct dosages were critical, especially when intended for internal use. The therapeutic practice of *pani* brought closure to a treatment period, and it marked the end of dietary restrictions given to the patient. *Pani* often consisted of eating specific seafoods, presumably to strengthen the body.

Historically, there have always been great challenges in herbal medicinal practices in Hawai'i. In ancient times, practitioners lacked access to references outside their immediate area. Although they had detailed chants and traditions, they did not have written medical reference texts seasoned over thousands of years, like those of the Chinese that date back to 3000 BC. Hawaiian practitioners had well-developed intuitions but also abundant superstitions. Once foreigners began arriving, particularly the European sailors, the native Hawaiian population was slashed by the tens of thousands. By the mid-1800s, in the wake of the contagious epidemics that were sweeping through Hawai'i, native practitioners began doubting the effectiveness of their traditional remedies, which were virtually powerless against such mighty plagues as smallpox and cholera.

In 1867, Hawaiian practitioners held a large conference on Maui. They founded a group called the "Ahahui Laau Lapaau" (of Wailuku) to discuss what could be done to protect their people, and what role the traditional native practitioners and medicines should continue to have in health care. The de facto government's Department of Health had been established, taking on the self-appointed role of dictating all public health care matters to eliminate "sorcery" and disbar "quacks" from practicing. They wanted to correct the practices of "ungodly unenlightened nations" and instill higher standards of sanitation. It was a desperate situation for all, and these 21 native practitioners did some sincere and well-documented inquiries into the validity and practicality of their knowledge, as well as the legal and ethical consequences of their continued practice.

The legislature passed an act to establish a Hawaiian Board of Health, signed by Kamehameha V, on June 23, 1868. Licenses were issued for $10 and later for $20 under "Papa Ola Hawaii," the board under King Kalakaua. But the foreign members still blamed the high Hawaiian mortality rates on the "inferior" Hawaiian medicines, and within a few decades, the laws of the Euro-Americans had taken over the entire kingdom. Although all licenses were thereby voided, the Bishop Museum archives contain writings confirming the continuation of traditional practices done in secret. The clear disdain expressed by the naturalized citizens of the de facto government over their lack of control of the native people is enlightening as to their self-serving motives.

A fascinating report of these events was published in 1994 in Malcolm Naea Chun's book titled *Must We Wait In Despair*. Many native practitioners organized, identified, and documented their cures and testimonials to present to the Board of Health "for the good of all so that [traditional practitioners] can practice." They had hoped that the Board would begin certifying native practitioners, but they also believed it was their duty to carry on regardless. The practitioners, aged from 27 to 63, had been trained in *hāhā*, childhood illnesses, *nānā maka* (visual observation skills), *mōʻike* (dream interpretation), and, occasionally, in "black magic."

Two very knowledgeable native Hawaiian herbalists on the island of Hawai'i today are Kai Kaholokai (of Kawaihae, above left) and Ikaika Keahiolaikaikaotalani Dombrigues (of Hilo, right). They learned from the old masters who have since passed away, like Kahuna *pule* David "Kawika" Kaalakea, Kahu Harry Mitchell, Uncle Tommy Soloman, Papa Henry Auwae, and Kalua Kaiahua, just to name a few.

Kai has also studied Ayurvedic Medicine, and classifies both illnesses and the local plants based on their elemental properties (bitter, sweet, salty, etc.). When not teaching, he grows herbs at home and makes unique remedial formulas.

Because of the serious misinformation of true Hawaiian indigenous history and culture, Kahuna Ikaika remains steadfast in maintaining the teachings exactly as they were handed down to him. "The knowledge that was imparted to me was *kapu*, therefore I resist the modern commercialism of selling herbs and the healing that comes from *Ke Akua.*"

Respect is also due to the great teachers throughout the islands, including Richard Kekuni Blaisdell, MD, his niece Nalani Minton, Alapai and William Kahuena, Kalama Makaneole, Kapiiohookalani Lyons Naone, Papa I'i, Levan Ohai, June Gutmanis, Ken Kamakea, Bill and Rachael Kanekoa, Joseph and Kaipo Kaneakua, and Joe Hamakua.

There are hundreds of Hawaiian medicinal substances and many good books available about them. The full Hawaiian names often described the color, growth patterns, or characteristics of the plants. Where a plant grew, if it was alone or in a group, how and when it was gathered or harvested, how perfectly it was formed, and how well the accompanying *kapu* was honored or *oli* was recited—all of these factors were believed to affect the potency of the medicine.

Because of their power and potency, please do not experiment with plants and medicines, especially for internal use. Seek the advice of an expert or herbal physician first.

There are many indigenous (native) and endemic (unique to Hawai'i) nurseries and propagation programs now run by both private and public agencies that sell many of these plants, as well as numerous reforestation projects to both promote native plants and irradicate invasive alien species.

The following is a summary of some of the most common and popular plants used in the Hawaiian healing arts in both ancient and modern times. Many are recognized as "migration plants" because the Polynesians brought them on their canoes to Hawai'i over great distances.[13] The following descriptions come from many sources, both written and oral. Notes are included at the back of the book to credit some of these sources.

- **'Awa** (*Piper methysticum* / kava). Relaxing and analgesic, a drink made from the roots and water or coconut milk was used for headaches, insomnia, lung troubles, and anxiety. Usually drunk in *'apu 'awa* (coconut shell cups), it was the drink of choice after hard work. Fermented, it can be intoxicating. A sacred ceremonial drink, it was an appropriate offering to the gods.

- **'Awapuhi** (*Zingiber zerumbet* / wild ginger). The roots or underground stems have uses for both food and medicine. Raw or cooked, it is renowned for its digestive, antibacterial, and antiviral effects. It also helps rid the body of parasites.

- **'Ilima** (*Sida fallax* / lantern flower). The delicate orange flowers, occasionally found in leis, were also chewed for female disorders or as a mild laxative. The bark of the roots can be a tonic.

- **Kalo** (*Colocasia esculenta* / taro). Shown above, *kalo* was and is one of the most important plants of Polynesia. The leaves and roots of some 30 (dry and wet) varieties were a staple food. The roots of some varieties were grated raw into mixtures as a laxative. The cut stems can be used to soothe insect bites.[14] *Poi* (mashed *taro*) is a prized, highly digestible food for babies or anyone who cannot assimilate milk or other foods.

- **Kī** (*Cordyline terminalis* / ti). The *ti* plant is a popular choice for landscaping, especially around homes because its *mana* can help offer protection. The juice and tea from the roots, flowers, and young leaves were healing to the lungs and used to cleanse the colon.[15] In more modern times, an intoxicating drink from the root called *'ōkolehao* was made. Cool, wet leaves are deboned and used across the forehead to reduce a fever. Leaves are also used with hot stone massage, shiny side against the skin. The leaves are excellent for wrapping and steaming foods.

- **Kō** (*Saccharum officinarum* / sugar cane). Often used to sweeten bitter-tasting medicines, the fresh juice or sap from the cane stalks is healthy, unlike when refined and bleached into its table-sugar, crystallized form. The Hawaiians chewed and sucked on the inner part of the stems.

- **Koʻokoʻolau** (*Bidens spp.* / Spanish needle). A popular tonic today, the leaves are marketed commercially as a tea. It is known for its positive effects on debility and gout.[16] An abundant weed, it can be used to help colon and liver problems.[17]

- **Kuawa** (*Psidium guajava* / guava). High in vitamin C and calcium, it is a popular fruit in juices, jellies, and jams. The juice from the leaf buds is also used externally for sprains and injuries, as well as internally for diarrhea. The roots were pounded, simmered, strained, and then drunk to stop bleeding in the bowels.[18] It also can be used for nerve and musculoskeletal aches.[19] Too much can cause constipation.[20]

- **Kukui** (*Aleurites moluccana* / candlenut). Every part of this mighty tree (shown above) was used. The raw kernels of the nuts were used as a purgative; the baked and pounded meat for ulcers, enemas, mouthwash, and skin sores.[21] The sap, bark, leaves, and blossoms are also of value for thrush, *tapa* dyes, skin disorders, and enemas.

- **Limu** (*Sargassum echinocarpum* / seaweed). Tender *limu* from the ocean and freshwater ponds is as popular today as it was in ancient times. High in minerals, it is a blood tonic and popular addition to *poke* (raw fish dishes). Externally, it was applied to increase circulation.[22]

- **Lūkini** or **wapine** (*Cymbopogon citratus* / lemongrass). A popular plant originally from Indonesia, it grows in Hawai'i and is used often in soups and as a tea. It is also a remedy for stomach, colon, bladder, bowel, and liver problems.[23]

- **Mai'a** (*Musa sp.* / banana). A nutritious food, the vitamin-rich sap from the large flower bud was used for digestive disorders and cramps.[24] There are many varieties of bananas today, eaten both raw and cooked.

- **Māmaki** (*Pipturus spp.*). A very tasty tea, this herb is marketed commercially today as a general tonic. In ancient times the bark was used for *tapa* cloth. It can be used for problems with the liver, bladder, and bowels.[25]

- **Niu** (*Cocos nucifera* / coconut). In addition to hard coconut meat and milk that is readily available today, the water and "spoon meat" from the young coconut was used for food and medicine, often in recipes for colds.[26] It is also good for diabetes, high blood pressure, colon cleansing, and kidney and liver problems. Every part of the *niu* had uses, including the shell, husk, leaves, trunk, and nuts.[27] Shown above is a cut green coconut, ready to scoop out the soft, delicious *kaniuhaohao* (spoon meat).

- **Noni** (*Morinda citrifolia* / Indian mulberry). A powerful antioxidant, the yellow fruit is high in terpene compounds and vitamin C. The leaves can be heated over an open flame or electric burner, then placed over sprains and strains to speed healing. The unripe green fruit is pounded and mixed with salt as a poultice for broken bones, or the ripe fruit is mashed as a poultice for infections, tumors, and hair loss in young  people.[28] *Noni* juice is beneficial for high blood pressure and the elimination of lice and worms. Usually the smelly, ripe fruit is fermented in gallon jars in the sun for months before it is ready. Alternatively, the fruit can be mashed fresh as a "smoothie" or an iced slush and stored in the refrigerator to make it a tastier drink.[29] For some conditions, it can be too acidic and should be avoided.[30] The roots were used for a yellow dye.

- **ʻŌlena** (*Curcuma domestica* or *longa* / tumeric). A powerful antiseptic and anti-inflammatory agent, this root is used medicinally for bleeding ulcers, sinus infections, and earaches. This "eye, ear, nose, and throat" medicine also provided an orange dye, which was frequently used in blessings and *hula* altars.

- **Pia** (*Tacca leontopetaloides* / Polynesian arrowroot). The tubers are prepared and dried as a powder and used in many recipes for dysentery and diarrhea.[31]

- **Pōpolo** (*Solanum nigrum* / black nightshade). These wild black berries contain poisonous alkaloids. The young leaves are used as a food or cold remedy.[32] Small quantities of the leaves and berries can strengthen the immune system and treat blood pressure disorders, as they build red blood cells.[33]

• **Pua aloalo** (hibiscus flower). A popular remedy for boils, the young, unopened buds are used before going into labor to assist in childbirth.[34] Today it is the official state flower of Hawai'i.

• **'Uala** (*Ipomoea batatas* / sweet potato). The tubers are used either raw as a gargle for sore throats or cooked as a nutritious food. Today the purple variety, usually grown on Moloka'i, is popular.

• **'Ulu** (*Artocarpus altilis* / breadfruit). Another staple food, the large starchy fruits are either eaten when ripe and soft or cooked like potatoes when hard. The sticky, milky sap was used for skin problems, cuts, or sores in the mouth. It was pounded into *poi,* especially when *taro* was unavailable. The tree trunks were used for canoes, drums, and surfboards.

Other *Mea Lapaʻau*

In addition to botanicals, the Hawaiians regularly used various animal and mineral substances for their medicinal properties. Some of these are listed below:

• **'A'ama** (black crab). Sucking the meat and juices from the raw, black crab is considered quite a delicacy. Another general word used for a crab is *pāpaʻi.*

• **'A'awa** (wrasse fish). Many varieties of fish were used, and many fish were bred in shoreline fishponds for accessibility and freshness.

• **'Alaea** (red ocherous earth). Rich in colloidal iron, it was often used for anemia and hemorrhage. It is useful for mothers who have just given birth and for cancer or AIDS.[35] As a blood builder (red blood cells), Hawaiians put a quarter teaspoon in water and drink it, making sure the source is pure.[36] *'Alaea* (often mistakenly called *alae*) is used to make Hawaiian red salt (below), popular in cooking and in *lomilomi* treatments. Essential oils can also be added to the salt, which then gets dissolved into warm water, dispursing the oils.

- **Hāʻae** (human saliva). High in enzymes essential for the proper digestion of starches, *taro, ʻulu*, and sweet potatoes were often pre-chewed for the *keiki* (children).

- **Heʻe** (squid). The *ʻalaʻala* ("ink bag" in the head) was roasted over the fire, mixed with *kukui* nut relish, and eaten as a highly nutritious food.[37]

- **Honu** (green sea turtle). The lean and nutritious meat was regularly eaten like any fish, but the fat was of particular value for skin ailments and burns. The shell was used medicinally. Once abundant, foreigners overfished and exported the meat until the turtle was endangered. Now laws protect the turtle, and populations are increasing.

- **Hua** (eggs). A few references are found regarding the use of chicken and spider eggs.

- **Huʻa kai** (sea foam). This was used to add moisture and saltiness to various preparations.

- **ʻIna or wana** (sea urchins). In addition to this short-spine variety known as Aristotle's lantern, there were several others.

- **Lānahu** (charcoal) and **lehu** (wood ashes). Both of these substances were used to give texture to formulas.

- **Lepo** (soil). Soil was used from either iron-rich *'alaea* sources or from a *lo'i* (*taro* patch).

- **Mimi** (urine). Sometimes urine was mixed with rock salt in poultices for sprains.[38] Some say it also counteracts alkaline stings (like from jellyfish).

- **'Ōpae** (shrimp). Found in rivers and brackish ponds, it is a popular medicinal food.

- **'Opihi** (limpet). A highly valued food (similar to oysters) that grows on coastal rocks, it is a very nutritious and expensive delicacy. In ancient times, the soft part was mixed with *poi* and sweet potatoes for the diet of a child (at six months of age).[39]

- **Pa'akai** (salt). There were and are many, many uses for Hawaiian sea salt in food and medicine preparation. In water, it makes an excellent gargle for sore throats.[40] It was also used in heat application; the rock salt was dry fried, wrapped in a cloth or towel, and used as a hot pack over sore muscles and rheumatism.[41]

- **Wai** (freshwater). In addition to rivers and waterfalls, it can refer to any liquid except *kai*. *Wai lani* describes pure rainwater held in the *taro* leaves; *wai puna* refers to springwater.

- **Wai kai** (salt water). Salted water has many practical uses. As an internal cleanser, *kai* (seawater) is diluted with *wai*. Once it matches the pH of the body, it is neither absorbed by nor leached into the body, making it an effective purgative.[42]

- **Waiū** (milk). A good oil-soluble medium for formulas, it was particularly nutritious for the young and the weak.

There are many excellent books available on Hawaiian plants and medicines. For more information, I highly recommend visits to the Bishop Museum archives, botanical parks, universities, museums, and libraries in Hawai'i.

ʻIke ʻia nō ka loea i ke kuahu.

An expert is recognized by the altar he builds.

It is what one does and how well he does it

that shows whether he is an expert.

~7~

Healing Practitioners

Kāhuna and Practitioners

There were several masters, healers, and doctors in most Hawaiian villages, but the most famous is the *kahuna*. A *kahuna* (plural, *kāhuna*) is a master or expert in a particular field of study or craft, which became his or her life's purpose. This includes the doctors, architects, scientists, agriculturists, prophets, navigators, carvers, and many healers and artisans. In the old times, they were often priests or honored as spiritual elders. L. R. McBride states in his book *The Kahuna* that they were the masters of specific subjects who "devolved the responsibility of conserving resources, advancing knowledge, and meeting new situations within the framework of natural laws and human nature."

These natural laws included universal laws, and the knowledge they carried was full of both authentic power and great responsibility. Persons of real ability (based on lineage, intelligence, talent, dedication, worthiness, and willingness to learn) were chosen to learn and carry on a particular skill. They would spend decades training, spending endless hours observing their *kumu* at work in order to perfect their skills. This in itself was a type of ordination, as these occupations were not self-chosen as careers are today.

Pule was an essential ingredient in all *kāhuna* practices, and it remains the secret behind their authentic power. The Bishop Museum archives contain writings that refer to the ability of *kāhuna* to "perceive the sex of the child the *hāpai* (pregnant) mother was carrying by clairvoyant means, in a state of trance, or through revelation in a dream." Other writings say, "the period of gestation has always been regarded as fraught with risk from malevolent psychic influences for mother and child." The works of a *kahuna ʻanāʻanā* might be negated in this case by the superior counteracting medicine and *pule* of the *kahuna kāhea.* McBride notes, "Their prayers were the focus of force emanating from their being."

Skills were mastered by memorizing fantastic amounts of information, often in the form of poems and chants. *Kāhuna* would align themselves with their *ʻaumākua* and ancestors through their flawless performances to increase their personal *mana.* Historians consider these ancient prayers and chants among the finest in the world because of their graceful rhythms, vivid imagery, and tremendous depth of meaning with all their literal, historical, and legendary references.

Fishermen and farmers, for example, had to learn the lunar influences on crops, weather, and fishing seasons. They had to memorize the rising and setting points of more than 120 stars and know their changes in position throughout the year. Each change of the wind and kind of rain also had a name, denoting its character, strength, or direction. Meteorologists had to observe the predictable ways the winds altered direction and force, or the behavior of birds and animals before various weather patterns. All reference information and all testimonials and stories from the past had to be orally memorized.

The healers knew hundreds of herbal remedies and many techniques for enhancing wellness. Besides *lomilomi* massage practitioners, who were called the *kāhuna lomilomi,* there were many other types of *kāhuna* and wisdom keepers, including the *kauka* (doctor), *kupuna* (elder or ancestor), *kahu* (guardian), and *kumu* (teacher). For a detailed list, please consult the glossary.

The *kahuna* was rich in *mana.* Without *mana,* skills were limited to purely human levels. Greg Scott encourages all practitioners to increase their *mana* before beginning the massage. "Without *mana,*" he writes, "*lomilomi* is just a lot of rubbing." For tips on how to increase your *mana,* please see chapter 3.

The profiles presented (in random order) on the following pages spotlight a few elders and specialists practicing and teaching the Hawaiian healing arts on the Big Island at the end of the twentieth century. There are many more, especially in the field of herbal medicine. Some accept their *kāhuna* status, while others prefer to use more modern Christian concepts to explain their skills. Nonetheless, these elders have served as living treasures in the world of Hawaiian *lomilomi* and healing. "Talking story" is a local term for just hanging out and chit-chatting with someone, as these are not formal interviews or biographies.

TALKING STORY WITH

Aunty Margaret Machado

FOR MOST OF HER ADULT LIFE, the renowned Margaret Kalehuamakanoelulu'uonapali Machado could be found in South Kona surrounded by visitors, family, and students. She has taught and healed countless students and patients from around the world. For

many years, she had been teaching her "last workshop" in Hawaiian *lomilomi* until her age and health inspired her to retire to her Kainaliu home several years ago. Classes, today led by her daughter Nerita, are filled with a group of students who opt to spend almost a month living and learning *'ohana* style by the sea.

On an aged and weathered porch across from a rocky beach south of Kealakekua Bay, students from all walks of life have learned how to give a full-body massage and cleanse the body of parasites and toxins. The porch is usually adorned with flowers, a beautiful portrait of Aunty, and large drawings of the human body with arrows and routine patterns. A poster-sized prayer titled "My God and I" reminds us that "God and I will go unendingly . . . in the field together," walking and talking as good friends, and as we "grasp our hands, our voices ring with laughter."

Aunty is a living legend of loving touch, and her humble nature is steadfast. During one visit, I found her sitting in the kitchen in between classes. People popped in constantly. A student of three years ago was preparing salad for all the workshop attendees. A niece was visiting. Another former student was "just passing through" and had brought some delicious fruit. Another friend was cooking a main course for everyone, asking, "How is this, Aunty?" I arrived with some *lehua* blossoms[43] from Volcano, located on the other side of the island, and they were added with great appreciation to the many vases of fresh flowers on the porch. Luckily, she is blessed with many devoted friends and family members to assist her in all her daily affairs.

She gave me a few uninterrupted moments that day, and we discussed the days gone by when we spent our years teaching in Kona back in the 1980s and when we received our state massage licenses by massaging the Board of Massage "judges" way, way back in the 1960s and 1970s. At that time, massage therapists did not need any formal schooling before taking the state exams as they do now. Aunty received license number MAT-303, and I received number MAT-697—now the licenses are numbered 7000+.

When the discussion came to Huna shamanism and the ancient Hawaiian healing arts, she simplified things: "There is only one God, and he does all the healing." A devoted Seventh-Day Adventist, she believes that *pule* enables God's soul to reach out to yours and the

Lord's healing to flow through you both. "If your hands are gentle and loving, your patient will feel the sincerity of your heart." She also stresses forgiveness through *ho'oponopono,* the "art of mental cleansing by the use of discussion, examination, and prayer." She received her healing powers from her grandfather John "Ko'o" Au, who was very skillful in *ho'oponopono,* and, in her words, from Lord Jesus.

Today her students are teachers and practitioners in their own right. Her longtime student and assistant instructor Glenna Wilde, a naturopath, passed away in the summer of 2002 after many years of devoted service to Aunty, particularly in the internal cleansing courses. When Aunty began teaching in 1973, she was criticized by the Hawaiian community for openly sharing *lomilomi.* But she always felt it was her divine calling, and it has been through her efforts that *lomilomi* was a leading part of the resurgence of interest in native Hawaiian healing. Many of her students began apprenticing with her in the 1970s and early 1980s, like Maka'ala Yates, Ka'ohu Monfort-Chang, Lisa Candelero, Danielle Coakley, Rae Ho'okano, Tamara Mondragon, Mary Golden, and the late Steven Bogardus, to name a few.

Many students can remember when Aunty, while in her prime, would look right through us, into our hearts and souls, reading us like a book. She would look right past the physical complaints and speak to our deepest hurts, fears, and thoughts. Her loving gifts will always live on in those who have been blessed to know and love her.

*R*ECIPE FOR 10-DAY SALTWATER CLEANSING

as taught (with great humor and sincerity)
by the late Glenna Wilde, ND

To truly heal, people need to remove themselves from their stressful lifestyles, get plenty of rest, and surrender to the cleansing process. Let others prepare the meals and formulas. Increasing knowledge leads to empowerment and motivation to heal yourself as well as reducing any shame or embarrassment. The fecal excretions of the body reveal the truth of the state of the small and large intestines, and thus the blood and overall health of the individual.

EAT – Fresh enzyme and high-fiber foods like salads, papayas, raw fruits and vegetables, etc., in preparation.

DAILY – Pray. (We would get up at 6 a.m.) Exercise and sunbathe. Go walking and swimming.

Go outside and let your eyes absorb beauty! Take steam baths (alternate hot and cold) to increase elimination via the skin. Finish with a swim in the ocean, if possible.

DRINK – Saltwater formula: Mix 1/3 *kai* (clean ocean water) with 2/3 *wai* (pure freshwater).

Lemon and cayenne pepper can be added. Drink in steam bath to replenish minerals.

On the second day drink a psylium-bentonite formula to absorb all fecal matter in the pockets of the large intestine. After the first week, you can use small sections of the stems of *koali* (blue morning glory) to boil and make a tea. This wrings out the internal organs like a sponge, cleansing the liver, as does castor oil.

MASSAGE – Gravity is not our friend! So we lie inverted on a slant board, and on the left side. This helps the ascending and (usually prolapsed) transverse parts of the large intestine (also known as the colon), respectively. Massage the abdomen in a clockwise direction with the knees bent to help dislodge fecal matter. Use castor oil, which goes into the lymphatic system and is both antiviral and antimicrobial.

TALKING STORY WITH

Uncle Kalua Kaiahua

IT WAS RARE TO SEE Kaluaokalanipaea Kaiahua without a big smile on his face. He was a walking, talking encyclopedia of jokes, sayings, and stories laced with wisdom to remind us who we really are. Although he passed on in August 2000, he left behind many small publications and dozens of well-trained apprentices who are actively carrying on his work.

Uncle Kalua was born on Moloka'i and raised in Kalihi, on O'ahu. His father was an herbalist and his mother was a nurse. All his

life, his mission was to advance the Hawaiian healing practices "through providing integrated Hawaiian and Western healing arts in a caring, professional, and ethical manner." In combining old and new healing methods, he used herbs, lava rocks, massage, humor, *aloha*, and more humor. He also spent many years teaching courses in Hawai'i, the US mainland, and Europe designed to reconstruct the body, mind, and spirit.

Uncle Kalua loved to sing and play guitar.

Uncle Kalua was a well-known *kupuna*, as he had frequently traveled with the support of his wife Annette, who was his business manager. He retired to his home on Maui in 1999 where a constant stream of people dropped by for a dose of his *aloha*. He always treated his clients' spirit in addition to their physical bodies. "The seed of success," he said, "is in our state of mind." This statement captured his working knowledge of *ho'oponopono*, the body-mind technique of making things correct or setting things straight. His parents taught him *lā'au lapa'au* and treatments with simple home remedies. He originally learned about healing touch from his blind aunt, Annie Uesugie. In the old style, she taught him how to turn a breech baby in the womb and how to treat colicky babies. She also told him to turn to God: "Wisdom, knowledge, and understanding come from God." Uncle practiced this consistently his whole fruitful life.

TALKING STORY WITH

Aunty Mary Fragas

BEING IN AUNTY MARY'S presence is an experience in loveliness. Her voice, gestures, and mannerisms are soft and sincere. Like many *kūpuna*, she has a steadfast faith in God. Her *lomilomi* primarily consists of praying and inspiring others to live a pure life. She is a firm

believer in internal cleansing, sharing that she "thoroughly cleanses herself every six months." She encourages others to do the same.

Aunty is unique in that she is self-taught through her own life experiences. When she was only six, she was suddenly stricken with infantile paralysis along with 23 other children at their school in Honoka'a. In 1929, the doctors did not understand what polio was, and during her examinations, she was unable to move her arms and legs. Many of her classmates died. Her parents began a daily routine to improve her circulation. They wrapped her every day with blankets soaked in hot water, massaged her skin with friction movements, and gave her a lot of love. She remembers always feeling cold, even at the low elevation of her home. "Six doctors gave up on me back in 1929, and now they are all dead and I am still alive!" Aunty notes. Now at 76, she happily helps others at her Hilo home.

For many years she devoted a lot of effort and struggle to get on her feet and return to school. She worked with the telephone company for years and later met and married her late husband. "We had five

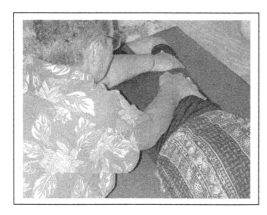

wonderful children during our years together. I wondered how he could love anyone in my condition," she confides, "but he did." He never saw her as a cripple. He "just loved me."

She began massaging others in 1948. Everyday she prays for guidance "to help the people who come" to her. She bought many books about illnesses, massage techniques, and the human body, which she describes as "this most interesting form of creation which God has provided for us." Her upper-body strength allows her to massage the many people who visit her. Although she can stand and walk a little, she prefers working on a mat on the floor. She unsuccessfully tried several times to pass the state massage-licensing exam, but then changed her mind. "God told me, 'What you know is not your own,' so I just let God help me to help people."

TALKING STORY WITH

Papa Henry Auwae

IN HIS NINETIES, Poʻokela Kahuna Lāʻau Lapaʻau o Hawaiʻi Papa Henry Allen Auwae still kept busy doing blessings and traditional healing on the Big Island. In October 2000, the last time I saw him, he

was one of many fascinating featured speakers at an indigenous healing conference in Waimānalo, Oʻahu. Then peacefully on December 31, 2000, the eve of the true millennium, he "walked the rainbow" to join his ancestors, wife, and several of their deceased *keiki.*

A true master in Hawaiian herbal medicine and healing, Papa Auwae's vast knowledge and experience was impressive. He was born in 1906 in Kokoʻiki, Kohala, and began to learn Hawaiian medicine at the knee of his great-great-grandmother when he was seven years old. He has taught and counseled tens of thousands of people from around the world, including many Western physicians. He established medicinal herb gardens at Queen's Medical Center and trained practitioners in spiritual and herbal healing techniques in hospital settings, including the holistic North Hawai'i Community Hospital, in

Kamuela. It was not unusual for physicians to consult Papa for insight into their problematic chronic cases.

During his blessings of homes and offices, Papa would use dried yellow bamboo and red 'alaea (Hawaiian mineral salt), scattering it as he walked around the site asking the dark spirits to leave. Salt is renowned throughout Hawai'i for its cooling and purifying properties. A practicing Catholic, he harmoniously embraced both traditional Hawaiian and Christian practices.

After many years in Keaukaha near downtown Hilo, he spent most of his time in the Kohala region in the north part of the island, which today is dry and windy compared to wet, windward Hilo. Papa would tell us stories when Kohala was different. "Long ago, when I was younger, there were sugar plantations here and the water flowed, filling the Hāpuna stream." Hāpuna Beach, now a state park and one of the world's most beautiful white sand beaches, is located in a barren lava rock desert. Yet the word hāpuna means "spring that gives forth life." Kohala is the northwest district of Hawai'i island. Along this coast, stretching from Kohala to Kailua-Kona, there is a very long "King's Trail," numerous brackish ponds, and brilliant turquoise lagoons accessible only by boat or miles of hiking.

Many years ago in Hilo, Papa shared fresh cuttings of his favorite Hawaiian medicinal herbs, talking about the benefits of each one with a group of my apprentices. Then he went on to demonstrate his massage techniques. The strongest memory Papa left me was the quality of his touch. His hands were firm and strong, but his touch was soft like clouds. Although he never wanted to have a book written about his work, he left behind several devoted students who spent years training with him. He also chose one of his grandchildren to pass on his gift of healing *mana*, and she feels he will appear to her in her dreams when she is ready to share his wisdom with the next generation.

TALKING STORY WITH

Papa Sylvester Kepilino

SOMEWHERE BETWEEN an enigma and a lovable pet, Papa K. suddenly appeared one day, coming by my Hilo school often to talk story and share his *manaʻo*. Then he would disappear for months, a bit like a gypsy, popping up now and then, full of surprises.

Born in 1928, he was given the name Kiliwelu Ka Maka Iki Aliʻi Paʻakaula Kamoa-moa, which is roughly translated as "one with a soft and tender skin and the eyes of the seeing chief, with a strong line, and keeper of the vast lands." He was later baptized as Sylvester Kepilino.

Papa grew up in Ho'okena. He was raised by his grandfather, John Pa'akaula. He learned *lapa'au* using the *hā* (the breath of life) to heal bones from his father, "Old Man Sylvester," who died in 1952. One day papa took my arm to show me the *hā*, making a scooping gesture with his hand after exhaling "haaaa" into my forearm. I felt a wave of energy pass through my skin and tissues down to the bone. This technique, he explains, can also be done over long distances. In fact, it works on the same principles as *'anā'anā*.

Papa laughs often, sings beautifully, and seems to have solid ties with the *'āina* that are timeless, particularly the Big Island. On one trip to Hawai'i Volcanoes National Park, he showed us how to prepare a sacred *ho'okupu* with *ti* leaves. He has taught us many old prayers and how to use Hawaiian salt water in a massage.

Like many elder Hawaiians, he suffers from numerous health problems. In recent years he has been in and out of the hospital many times. During one stay, he had occasional visitors. "Two owls kept checking up on me." Papa believes the *pueo* owl is his family's *'aumakua* (guardian spirit). One time I saw him pass by an owl statue and break out in "chicken skin." As with many elders and healers, communicating with nature and animals is commonplace.

Papa K. lost his first wife many years ago. "She was an angel, so open-hearted," he recalled. After serving in the army in Germany and twelve long years of courtship, he and his sweetheart, Bonnie Domain, were married in Honolulu in 1965. They honeymooned in Las Vegas, where he spent 18 years as a chef. He "gave up" on many things after losing his wife to cancer in 1978. He returned to Hawai'i in 1987, spending many years teaching the Hawaiian language, making commercials for local television, and later doing *lomilomi*. He remarried in 2003 and now lives in Hilo.

Illustration showing the learning and practicing of hāhā diagnosis.

TALKING STORY WITH

Kauka Dane Ka'ohelani Silva

DANE KA'OHELANI SILVA was born and raised in Hilo in 1946. His long career as a *kauka* (doctor) and massage therapist began in 1979 as a native healer and apprentice under a holistic medical doctor. By 1986 he became a licensed massage therapist, and later a chiropractor and *lomi* instructor. His numerous auto and sports injuries

became the perfect learning journey to experientially understand the body's healing processes. When first licensed, he averaged 1,000 patients per year; today he is semi-retired and has cut that workload to about 350. In addition he now teaches *lomilomi,* primarily in Hawai'i and Japan, and heads the Hawaiian Lomilomi Association, which began holding annual educational conferences on the Big Island in 1999.

Honoring *nā kūpuna* and appreciating the *mana* of the Hawaiian Islands are an integral part of his teachings. "The *mana* of Hawai'i is undoubtedly the single most important aspect of the healing power of the islands." Cultivating this *mana* is key to one's personal success and health, as well as a necessary ingredient for healing one's self and others.

According to Dane, there are three basic and necessary components. "These are Akua (the Divine Creator), nature (land, sea, sky, animals, etc.), and people (you, me, and everyone else). When the person is in balance and harmony with Akua and Nature, then *ola* (life force) is accumulated. When this accumulation of life force is focused and directed, it becomes *mana*."

His main teachers taught him both Oriental and Hawaiian therapies and herbs. This leads to some interesting and unique treatment plans. For example, for one young client of his who was suffering from a severe case of systemic staphylococcus infection, the treatment protocol included topical applications of Tahitian *tamanu* oil and Chinese *yunnan paiyao* powder, Hawaiian *noni* leaf poultices and fruit skin scrubs, and *noni* juice taken internally in conjunction with Western antibiotics. "The outcome was excellent," he noted. Other treatments may incorporate deep massage and stretching outdoors or *lomilomi wai ola*—his aquatic massage therapy—that is done in a waist-high pool of warm water.

Kauka (doctor) Silva using kai to prepare a formula at Hilo Bay.

TALKING STORY WITH

Kumu Leina'ala K. Brown-Dombrigues

*H*E KUMU OLA (a living source), Leina'ala, a Hawaiian *mo'o* Lono *lomilomi lapa'au* healer and teacher, was trained by her *'ohana* since birth, and later by elders and *kāhuna lapa'au* since 1975. Born in Makiki and raised in Waimānalo on O'ahu, everything in her early

life was from the old style, including proper protocols for gathering seaweed, pounding *tapa* cloth, and daily reciting of various *pule* and *oli*.

Her lineage of teachers include Tūtū (grandparent) Ono (from Kaua'i), Tūtū Ida Kalua, (of Kekaha, Kaua'i), her mother Lorraine Leina'ala, her father Keliihoopii, Tūtū Emma Kaahuhailikaukoalaa, Uncle Alvin Isaacs (of O'ahu), and Uncle Lono, all of whom stressed the importance and power of *pule*. Some of this training was done at various *heiau* and while dancing *hula* with the Seven Sisters of Pele under Tūtū Charles Kenn and Abraham Kawai'i DeCambra.

It was Tūtū Kalua who gave her the diagnostic gift of *hāhā a me 'ōpū huli* (palpation of the abdomen), which is a sacred part of the family's *moʻokūʻauhau* (lineage). Her ancestors gave her the gifts of *lāʻau kāhea*, *hāhā*, and *hoʻo ʻōpū huli*. According to Leinaʻala, the *ʻōpū* is especially sacred, and *lomilomi* should never be misused in a sexual way as it is sometimes today. She furthered her training under Aunty Margaret Machado, Uncle Kalua, Uncle Harry, and Uncle Kawika. For spiritual and analytical balancing, Leinaʻala turns to Ginnie Kinney and master *hoʻoponopono* specialist Sonny Kinney. Today she blends Hawaiian *kāhuna lapaʻau* wisdom and herbal seawater cleansing programs with clinical medical therapy, which provides healing for the mind, body, and spirit.

Leinaʻala is a licensed massage therapist (LMT) and is certified in the state of Hawaiʻi to teach pre-licensing courses. She teaches courses in Volcano and in her Hilo clinic, the Hoʻōla ʻO Lomilomi Lapaʻau Clinic ʻO Hawaiʻi, and facilitates numerous educational workshops around Hawaiʻi island. For more than 25 years, she has been treating patients referred to her by doctors and individuals in Hawaiʻi and from around the world. "The cure always comes from within us," she explains.

Assisting and guiding her often was Aunty Abbie Napeahi, a well-known native Hawaiian *hoʻoponopono* specialist. A spiritual counselor and respected elder, she taught in the state of Hawaiʻi, training individuals, families, and the community the skills of *hoʻoponopono* and the simple keys to living in *lōkahi* (harmony). She passed away on January 31, 2005.

TALKING STORY WITH

Kauka Maka'ala Yates

BORN AND RAISED in South Kona, Maka'ala Yates has become a dynamic force and invaluable source in the Hawaiian healing arts today. He spent years studying with Morna 'Iolani Luahine and Edith Kanaka'ole, and moved to Oregon after more than 13 years of apprenticing with Aunty Margaret Machado, who lived in the same area he grew up in (Hōnaunau on the Kona coast near Captain Cook and Kealakekua Bay). He is a chiropractor and board member of the 'Ahahui Ho'ōla Hawai'i (Traditional Hawaiian Healing Council) and the Pacific Island Council of Traditional Healing.

He was born in Kona on June 23, 1948, and is a descendant of the Kipapa and Kekapahaukea lineage (of Kona and Maui). Intimate knowledge of the ancient ways was passed down to his father, John P. Yates.

Like his father, Maka'ala has an intimate connection with the ocean. His stories include the way his fisherman father would feed the adult *manō* (sharks) off the Kona coast to keep the younger sharks out of the area, tap the sides of the canoe to call the 'ōpelu fish to the surface, and "talk" with the dolphins.

Communicating with the spirit essence of things was part of the Hawaiian culture of old, he reminisces, because they were so con-

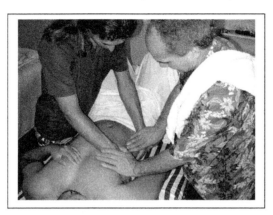

nected with nature every day of their lives. Hawaiians spoke with sincerity, meaning, and depth, which was something that impressed him deeply as a young man. Their culture stressed humility, and they were excellent caregivers of the 'āina. They gave unconditionally: What is mine is yours also! Today, he believes, the modernized lifestyle of the kānaka maoli has led to a disconnected and depleted culture. He is concerned about the lack of close bonds between the children and elders. "Teaching respect and honoring the kūpuna are critical for healthy communities. Without this, we are lost."

His own voyage to reconnect took him across the Pacific during the original sailing of the Hōkūle'a voyaging canoe back in 1976. He spent months on O'ahu with the crew, led by the renowned navigator Mau Piailug, preparing the vessel for the long trip down to Tahiti (French Polynesia). Then they were at sea for more than three weeks before being welcomed by hundreds of Polynesians in a very moving, powerful ceremony off the coast of Tahiti. This truly was a voyage of rediscovery, for it was about self-knowledge of his soul, and it opened the door to reconnecting the Hawaiians to their collective ancestral wisdom and mana.

Today he focuses his cultural teachings on a deep level to heal the individual as well as the entire planet by reconnecting to spirituality. "Who are you, deep in your soul?" he asks. "Whatever hurts you have, whatever is holding you back, get over it! Move on! Rediscover your soul qualities!" He believes people are *kānaka anela* (angelic humans), and that prayers should not ask for something but affirm it: "Abundant I am! *Pono* I am! This is the Hawaiian way."

He also believes in cleansing, and, as a Hawaiian *kauka* (doctor), he has written a book on ways to attain perfect health by proper diet, cleansing, fasting, and meditation. He knows that cleansing can help prepare people for changes, and he believes the planet is changing fast. "The planet's vibration is rising," and people need to make some hard and fast choices. "Now is the time to get back to the *'āina*, to live in gratitude, to release all limiting beliefs, and raise your vibration frequency."

Maka'ala teaches a series of *lomilomi* trainings throughout Hawai'i and the US mainland that include soothing but deep tissue massage, joint mobilizations, fasting programs, and the use of hot *'ili'ili* stones (heated in a roaster to exactly 130 degrees Fahrenheit) on the muscle tendons. Two of his favorite methods for cleansing the spirit and body include the *hā mo'o* (energizing the spinal column) meditation technique, and the *hale pūlo'ulo'u* (steam bath or sweat lodge, below) which he includes at the end of each course.

TALKING STORY WITH

Aunty Mahealani Kuamoʻo-Henry

MAHEALANI Kaiwikuamoʻokekuaokalani Henry (pictured with her husband Uncle Kamōʻī Henry) is a writer, artist, and teacher who shares with great joy the *aloha* spirit philosophy for *lōkahi* (harmony), self-awareness, and truth. A gifted native Hawaiian speaker from the dis-

trict of Puna, she is a *kumu ʻelele* (messenger) for the spiritual voices of her ancestors within the strong lineage of *nā kumu, kahu,* and *kāhuna* (trusted guardians, priests, advisors, and healers) under the leadership of Kaiwikuamoʻokekuaokalani, her ancestral *kupuna-kāne* (grandfather).

The ancient, spiritually-pragmatic teachings that date from about AD 342 to AD 1299 and their application in today's lifestyle are the focus of her unique method of *ho'oponopono*. In 1993, after fifteen years of teaching *hula* with her mother and sister in California, she began the public path to bring forward these ancient teachings of *ho'opono pono* (the second *pono* is separated from the first, which she translates as "making right, more right"), or what she calls *pono ke ala* (the right path). Both of these are more descriptive titles for the pre-Tahitian and pre-Western teachings that she refers to in her teachings and presentations.

In brief, *pono ke ala* involves the recognition and the permission that we give ourselves to accept our spiritual greatness and to experience it in our daily moments. Mahealani claims that her role as a teacher-messenger is easy because all she does is show up, and her ancestors do all the "messaging" at her presentations. It was the ancestors, or ancient ones, she explains, who placed the sacred beliefs and values in *kapu*, or protective restrictions—removed from the memory of the generations after AD 1299. It was the beginning of the foretold changes and influences upon Hawai'i *nei*. And the ancestors with infinite wisdom knew that the human dimension required experiences away from the oneness and greatness. According to Mahealani, a period of *na'aupō mana* (divine darkness) shall remain for a period lasting more than 600 years, they predicted. Once the human experience has filled itself and people choose to return to a state of *pono* (excellence/rightness), this divine darkness will pass.

In this line of *ho'opono pono*, one learns the value of "chicken skin" moments (also known as goose bumps). These special moments in life affirm that something is happening that transcends time and space, as we know it. It is a confirmation that there is another dimension of reality that lies a small step beyond what we think of as "normal" experiences.

Today she brings forward the teachings and methods that have been brought out of *kapu* to renew self-sufficiency and growth based in the timeless and healing concepts of *aloha lōkahi*. It is her hope that through the ancient teachings, the sacred beliefs and timeless values of the oneness and the greatness shall return to the memory of the people, and that the teachings be shared worldwide. Her teachings celebrate the *'uhane* as the spirit self and true identity. It is the essence of Hawaiian spirituality based in the pureness of the *aloha* spirit. And it is this spirituality that places the greatness and values in self, referred to as *mana iho* (self-greatness and doer) and *ka mea nānā i hana* (self as the mindful creator).

Mahealani served for years as a cultural-based counselor for a federal substance abuse rehabilitation program. Today she officiates at weddings, blessings, wakes, memorials, and other ceremonies as a "*kahu*-priestess."

TALKING STORY WITH

Daddy David Bray, Jr.

DADDY BRAY, JR., WAS a state-recognized *kahuna*. He had the power to make things happen. In his early years, he was a respected *kumu hula,* particularly with the *kāne* (male) dance troupes who were his *hula* students on O'ahu.

I first met David Ka'onohiokala Bray, Jr., when he was doing blessings on the Big Island in his later years. He and his wife came to my Kona massage school in 1989, shortly before he passed on. I planned the blessing as a traditional custom, never expecting any tangible results. I was surprised and delighted when things immediately changed following the ceremony. Prosperity soared, and things remained that way for quite some time. The results of his ceremony showed me that his connection with universal *mana* was very strong. Like his father, *kahuna* powers (from the *lapaʻau* order of

Kū) ran in his blood.

Our meeting took place near the ocean on very sacred, historically-rich royalty lands in Keauhou-Kona where one of my massage schools was formerly located. King David Kalakaua had a beach home there overlooking a bay with a breakwater that legend says was built by the *menehune* (legendary elf-like people). Daddy Bray was at one with the *mana* of the ʻāina and all the ancestral energies present there.

At the blessing of my Kona massage school, Daddy Bray set up an altar that included a feather cape and other power objects. He used *ti* leaves and chants with casual confidence. Afterward he joined us for food and laughter, accepting a small donation for his services.

Daddy Bray was familiar with the teachings of Max Freedom Long, and many of the pioneering Huna movement practitioners also studied with Bray. He was a true *kahuna kāhea.* He passed on several years before I wrote the first edition of this book, so he is the one elder presented on these pages with whom I never had an opportunity to share this project.

Ke ala iki a kāhuna.

The narrow path on which priests walk.

There are many restrictions to be heeded.

~•8•~

Interpretive New Age Styles

Temple Bodywork

Outside of the Hawaiian Islands, temple bodywork is the most common type of "Hawaiian massage" being done in the world. Its founder is the late Abraham Kawaiʻi DeCambra, who lived on Kauaʻi until he passed away in June of 2004. Although it is not traditional, it is accurate to say it is Hawaiian because a *kanaka maoli* man who was born and raised in Hawaiʻi developed it, as it is known today.

Today this style has flourished in Australia, Germany, and many other countries. Most of Abraham's students now teaching temple bodywork have modified it further, adding more hands-on techniques or their own versions of rituals and theories, which are often marketed as ancient Hawaiian rites-of-passage, tiki goddess worship, shamanic bodywork, *huna ka mana loa*, tandem temple *lomi, kahi loa, kahuna* bodywork, and sometimes as ritualistic, sexual initiations and transformations. In Germany, they use the term "Hawaiian healing" with a light, sensual massage to convey a feeling of paradise or a fantasy state of being.

According to his students, Abraham's teachings originally weren't about massage per se but about certain nonsexual sacred rituals and principles that were designed to increase personal *mana*. Abraham was trained in many *kahuna* arts, including *kaona* and *ho'okake*, which stress the use of one's innate perceptive abilities. In the late 1960s he was teaching *hula* and *lua* martial arts students deeper insights on how energy moves and how to master their movements with posture, positioning, placement, and rhythm. His early students explain that this included work on the individual's attitude and increasing *mana* and consciousness. His partner said that this is to empower "all those that have come before you, are now, and are yet to be." Later, the ancient teachings for performers of *hula* and *lua* evolved to the body being a "stage" and the bodyworker becoming the "performer."

Temple bodywork certainly produces profound results; recipients often describe them as life changing. On the positive side, people experience it as an uplifting genetic and spiritual experience. Many say that watching a temple-style massage demo "brought tears" to their eyes, and receiving it made them "cry like a baby." Others have had drastic adverse reactions, including attempts at suicide and requiring years of psychiatric counseling.

I personally have heard the full spectrum of reports, which seem to be directly related to the amount of sexual touching that occurs. Unless done in a mutually willing tantra session, recipients report they feel sexually violated.

Perhaps some can handle or desire a certain intensity these sessions bring, while others are so shocked that something shatters within them. A successful teacher of temple body-work told me that she, like most of the other female teachers, has dropped all sexual overtones from her work with very positive results. Male teachers, however, still seem to use more erotic and sexual techniques. One licensed therapist told me he witnessed a man massaging a nude woman in front of an audience; the performer finished by elevating her vagina toward the ceiling. "It was absolutely beautiful!" he assured me. Another man told me that after his wife received a session, she was so shaken that it took her months before she could even discuss it with him. Afterward, he was so shocked, he wrote me: "Is this really Hawaiian massage? It goes contrary to everything I ever knew about the Hawaiians."

In more than thirty years of living in the Hawaiian Islands, I have never seen or heard any trace of ritualistic sexual bodywork mentioned in any stories, chants, lectures, libraries, or *hālau hula.* Temple teachings (readily found on the Internet) claim that originally these *kahuna* arts were only taught and performed in the *heiau* (temples) and that Abraham "modified the methods to suit contemporary Western consciousness, to enable anybody to understand the Source of All." According to the Web pages of his top students, he was the "Kahuna through whose line all Kahuna trainings in non-Hawaiian Society" originated. Indeed, these teachings are primarily spread via non-Hawaiians, and most Hawaiians are usually flabbergasted when they learn of them. Others say that the students changed his teachings, but he did little to correct them.

Abraham, who used the name Kahu Auaʻia Maka ʻIʻole during the performance of sacred cultural rituals, never named any of his own teachers. Hoʻokahi, his surviving partner, who agrees that sexual overtones are inappropriate, told me that back in 1989 and 1990 when Abraham started teaching and traveling extensively, it was his students who gave his work the name "temple" to differentiate it from more "common" and traditional Hawaiian *lomilomi* techniques.

Since my calling has always been to honor the Hawaiian culture and uplift massage as a reputable health-care profession, I have not had a desire to follow this path as it is taught today. Nor have I found any evidence whatsoever after more than five years of research and travel amongst indigenous islanders in Hawaiʻi and Tahiti of any massage teachings of this nature being practiced anywhere in the Pacific islands before the mid-1900s. There is, however, much evidence that some of the body movements are similar to ancient forms of *lua* martial arts and *hula*. Many therapists, having no access to traditional ancient teachings, have cherished learning and sharing the temple style, and it has served as a doorway to open many hearts and as an opportunity for personal transformation.

Good advice to follow when one tries to understand the history and differences between traditional and temple styles of Hawaiian massage comes from Kauka Makaʻala Yates: "Discernment and *mālama pono* are probably the best pieces of advice I can give anyone regarding anything Hawaiian...The guidelines one should adopt when it comes to the Hawaiian culture or life in general is if the information resonates with your heart, mind, and spirit, then go with it. If it doesn't, then just chuck it out the window."

Huna Teachings

Today there are many inspiring and fascinating writings on Huna. Yet traditional *lomilomi* practitioners do not teach this philosophy. In fact, most insist that it is not from the native Hawaiian culture at all. How much of the ancient knowledge has been lost, and how much has been fabricated? A close look at the teachings of what is today referred to as the "Huna method" reveals many powerful truths about self-mastery and universal law. Yet why are so many Hawaiian elders disturbed about the "ancient Hawaiian teachings" of Huna?

Some historians believe that Max Freedom Long was the first to redefine and popularize the Hawaiian word *huna*. A schoolteacher who arrived in the Big Island's southern district of Ka'u in 1917, Long was a Caucasian who was fascinated with the study of psychology, the occult, and ancient magic systems. He attempted to understand the mysterious roles of the *kāhuna* and the then rarely-spoken Hawaiian language during a time when the culture was extremely suppressed due to foreign influences.

Long wrote his first book, *Recovering the Ancient Magic*, in 1936. Then in 1948, working out of his office in California, he wrote his second book and best seller, *The Secret Science Behind Miracles*, and a half dozen other books exploring Huna and the occult. He used the word *huna* to capture the principles behind some of the wisdom and power of the Polynesian peoples. In Long's own words, "The word for their secret lore was never found . . . it may have been too sacred to mention. The name we used, for this reason, was *Huna*."

Long had lived as a foreigner in a rugged, volcanic part of the island, far from any city, among a people he did not know, and he later attempted to explain things that were not discussed back then. The complexity of the Hawaiian language, as well as his unfamiliarity with the culture, limited his understanding. Once he had left the islands, he supplemented his brief experiences in Hawai'i with extensive research into the works of prominent psychologists, visionaries, and philosophers from around the world on such subjects as hypnotism, the ego, the subconscious mind, reincarnation, and the occult sciences.

Long received a huge response from his readers following his first book. Requests for self-help ideas poured in. He became an overnight authority for an anxious public longing for new answers, which probably led to much ongoing interpretive theorizing on his part. As sincere as he may have been in his research, Hawaiians claim that these ideas were primarily his own thoughts, not Hawaiian teachings from the Hawaiian people. His writings occurred during a period of Hawaiian history that forced the Hawaiians to place additional protective *kapu* on their traditional arts and sciences in order for them to survive foreign invasion, further adding to an air of mystery and secrecy. Long went on to write many more books, which were sold to tens of thousands of non-Hawaiians around the world, and the "Huna tradition" became a profitable, almost cult-like phenomenon by the mid-1900s. Many people sought out gurus throughout the late twentieth century, and they longed to gain the wisdom of the masters of India and the elusive *kāhuna* of Hawai'i.

While the word *huna* literally refers to a small or minute particle (like sea spray in *huna kai* or a drop of water in *huna wai*) it can also mean "hidden," as in a hidden object or secret. The word *hūnā* means "to hide or conceal." The word *kahuna*, which usually precedes a skill or subject (like *kahuna lomilomi*), can be defined in several ways. *Ka* (singular form of "the") and *huna* (small, secret, hidden) in *kahuna* is defined today as the "keeper of the secrets."

But another look suggests that a *kahu* (foundation; one who holds knowledge; sacred guardian) of *nā* (plural form of "the") followed by another word like *lomilomi* would be defined as "keeper of the art of *lomilomi* massage," which implies carrying on a great tradition of knowledge preservation, but not necessarily in secrecy. The destiny of the *kahu* was to make something his or her life's purpose. While the arts and skills were carefully mastered, kept, and passed down generation after generation, this definition makes more sense when referring to a *kahuna kalai* (master carver), for example.

Some knowledge and practices were placed in *kapu* for certain periods of time, or off-limits to commoners. And some say that certain knowledge, like *ho'ōla* or *ho'omake* (the medicine of life or death) or *'olohe* (an ancient martial art), was so powerful it could be very dangerous in the wrong hands. Misuse of power is nothing new; it has historically been the downfall of many great civilizations, and the Hawaiians were no exception. In fact, even today *kāhuna* sometimes succumb to spiritual power struggles.

Hawaiians tend to be extremely loving and generous, thus the term "Hawaiian hospitality." They are also, like all human beings, prone to corruption and greed. Some people feel that the majority of the native Hawaiians have yet to show an interest in *lomilomi* or truly integrate the inherent power and value of their noble ancestry. In fact, as a race, they are often described as chronically suffering from

"Polynesian paralysis." Many Hawaiians are very apprehensive or even fearful of returning to the old teachings and beliefs of yesterday. Foreigners have always found the Hawaiian people so "easy" to take advantage of, trick, and manipulate. Although they have been exploited for centuries, most Hawaiian people remain very humble, generous, and willing to share when approached with respect and sincerity.

In any case, to your average Hawaiian, the word *huna* usually refers to something that is small, insignificant, or obscured from view, if the term is used at all.

At certain points in Hawai'i's history, much knowledge was placed in hidden formats for specific periods for safekeeping. Sometimes there was so much dominance by the ruling class that the *kapu* system became excessive and controlling. People lived in constant fear. In fact, when the *kānaka maoli* hid in caves to escape slavery or death, many important teachings went underground, or their purity and power were lost and distorted. But during times of peace and great leadership, the healing arts were generally not "hidden" from the population. Many arts and sciences were valued and preserved for those who were worthy but not necessarily done in secrecy in the way some people define *huna* today.

There was no need to exaggerate the value or sacredness of certain teachings among the ancient people, as is frequently done today with Hawaiian massage. In fact, it is said that in ancient times everything was regarded as sacred. Everything and everyone had their place within one interconnected world. And some things were extra sacred and reserved for the very wise and learned. The telepathic skills of the *kahu* were awesome. If a villager sought out a *kahuna* for assistance in healing or for protection, the *kahuna* would probably be waiting, already knowing that someone was coming. Old chants and stories refer to ancestors who could ripen a stalk of bananas just with their thoughts. Much importance in Hawaiian society was placed on mental strengths, thought projection, memorization, telepathy, and self-mastery. Connecting deeply with the *mana* of the land and Akua, the Supreme Being, was and still is the "secret" to authentic power. It is told that at one time in Hawai'i, God's name was considered so holy that it was only expressed as a sacred vibrational sound pronounced "eeeee ohhhh."

Now we are faced with properly bringing knowledge out of protective *kapu* and applying the valuable teachings from the old ways. There is a good deal of dispute about the proper protocol for doing this. Huna may offer practical ways of attaining authentic power based on bits and pieces from indigenous practices. Often these concepts are described with Hawaiian words that are used in new, modern ways.

One of the powerful concepts of Huna is that simple ideas, when filled with "mesmeric force" (like *mana*) will cause reactions in oneself or in others (via the "low self" center of consciousness). Thus "force-charged" ideas and suggestions become powerful tools that are planted in the subconscious mind either by vocal or telepathic means. This low self then takes over, and the suggestion is put into action automatically. Huna teaches that for a suggestion to be effectively planted, the "middle self," or the individual's will, must be relaxed (or weak) enough to be mesmerized. One's middle self can give suggestions to one's lower self—the exact principle behind all autosuggestion techniques.

The universal truths behind these principles are still a subject of great mystery and fascination. Throughout the ages medicine men, shamans, priests, priestesses, rulers, and healers have used this method to overcome enemies, disease, and any thoughts preventing their desired outcome. No doubt this was the type of energy behind the effectiveness of the *kahuna kāhea*, the strength of the Polynesian warriors, the legendary *menehune*, and the power of the chanters of Molokaʻi who protected their island from foreign invasions. Today we often hear of the power of affirmations and subliminal messages to invoke change to our belief patterns, and of intention to increase the healing energies during a massage session.

The power of thought and the spoken word is a repeated theme in the Hawaiian healing arts. Modern physiology confirms that thoughts, memories, and emotions directly affect the neurotransmitters of the nervous system, which controls the entire body with continuous electrochemical actions and reactions. Esoteric teachings claim that unless a thought is consciously proclaimed that the subconscious patterns will take over. The *kāhuna* knew that thoughts have great substance. They also knew that thoughts traveled in ways that are not limited to time and space, as we know it. They did long-distance healings and always visualized the perfect state of health in the present moment of the healing sessions, regardless of the current state of the patient.

Human nature being what it is, there were and will always be some individuals with a lot of *mana* combined with self-serving wills who use the power of thought to harm or manipulate others for their own agendas, thus "black magic" or the "evil" *kahuna*. The residual *aka* cords, which subtly connect things and people to one another, serve as a cobweb-like telepathic conduit system. Unlike electricity that weakens over great distances, this *mana* can flow or remain static while never weakening throughout this perfect conductive medium. *Mana* is considered a living force, and it can be directed and redirected by intention. When this intention taps into the divine during *pule*, the potential is magnified immensely.

When the body is viewed in a holistic manner rather than merely a physical machine, one recognizes all levels of body, mind, and spirit. The subconscious (low self) and conscious (middle self) aspects give and draw energy to and from each other constantly. Enter the Divine Being, or Akua, with unlimited, unconditional energy and *aloha*, and a true correction or healing can manifest. *Pule* opens the door for infusing body and mind with spirit. Prayer is not a means of seeking or earning favor, nor is it reaching outside of one's self for the blessings of God or a higher power. More profound than our finite minds can conceive, it becomes a process of consciously arriving at a place in which we actually existed all along. Just because we are unaware of something does not mean that it does not exist. If God is omnipotent and omnipresent, where in the universe could there be a place where God is not present? Prayer, grace, and spirituality refer to states of "remembering" or "reconnecting" with God's presence. The quality of this energy is awesomely transforming, forgiving, and loving, thus the miraculous power of prayer and potency of *lomilomi* massage. Once the body, mind, and spirit are energized and harmonized, the individual has accepted full responsibility and love for himself or herself, and the conscious mind has embraced and surrendered to the indwelling divine presence, no disease or dysfunction will find a lasting home in that individual.

There is, has been, and probably will always be a great temptation to exaggerate the rarity and value of Hawaiian teachings, both by foreigners and Hawaiians. And it is perhaps for many self-serving reasons that the air of secrecy and allure of magic has become so extensively linked to various healing arts. The fascination of Huna is still very strong as readers seek universal truths flavored with the enchantment of the Hawaiian Islands. There is a growing number of practitioners who are making all sorts of claims about their abilities. As with all things, it becomes the individual's job to use discernment and not misuse the power.

While a teaching certainly does not have to be Hawaiian to be valuable, the Hawaiian people are generally uneasy with Huna teachings, especially those who have adopted a strict Christian view of life. *Kānaka maoli* are very sensitive to teachings that are labeled "ancient Hawaiian" that differ from their traditional practices, are promoted by non-Hawaiians, and lack reverence for their culture. Ironically, the native Hawaiian people themselves, most of whom were raised in schools run by foreigners, are not as interested in learning their own indigenous practices as are foreigners. And many foreigners are willing to pay big bucks. So now we are seeing a lot of *kahuna* trainings, Huna masters, and weekend *lomilomi* certification workshops that are quite surprising and saddening to the Hawaiian people, especially the elders. Most elders feel that these modern teachings lack the respect and safeguards that were present in the *'ohana* system, and they are puzzled by the new and strange usage of the old Hawaiian words. Others believe that modern attempts to understand and master the old teachings can help open the world's eyes to the beauty and value of Hawaiian culture, and bring the world much-needed skills for peace, self-mastery, and divine awareness.

One such teacher is Serge Kahili King. Serge is a master of positive thinking. He has spent years teaching people how to clear the mind of fears and unseen obstacles that keep them from achieving happiness and success. Drawing from a diverse background of African shamanism, psychology, and years living with the Polynesian peoples, he has created a comprehensive philosophy of universal truths that cross many cultural boundaries. His students now have students, and they have added their own perspectives, experiences, and beliefs to the Huna teachings. Taking over where Max Freedom Long left off, Serge's Aloha International member-ship boasts more than 10,000 members worldwide. He has extensive writings and videos about mystical revelations, communicating with the elements of nature, specific tools for shamanic development, enhancing psychic abilities, and the meaning of *aloha.*

Serge King leading a group in ceremony.

A portion of Serge's teachings deal with bodywork as taught by his longtime student, Susan Floyd. He calls this "Lomi Lomi Nui," and it consists of Huna teachings combined with temple-style massage techniques that Susan learned from Abraham. In response to my inquiry as to the extreme sexual nature of the temple style of *lomilomi* so prevalent today, Serge responded, "If there is sexual abuse by someone practicing the temple-style massage taught by Abraham, it is the action and responsibility of the practitioner, and not an inherent fault of the system. As you must know, anyone in a healer/client relationship may abuse his or her position if he or she does not maintain moral and ethical guidelines.

"Huna is a philosophy which promotes effectiveness over form, and therefore any techniques that work. Sometimes we say, 'If it works, it's Huna.' Also, since there are no limits, in our healing work we use the idea that you can change the body to heal the mind, and you can change the mind to heal the body. In addition, since now is the moment of power, any kind of healing always affects past, present, and future."

Major Bones of the Body

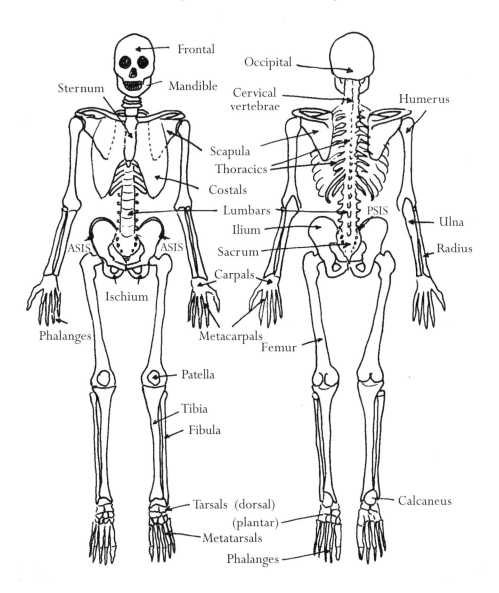

Major Muscles of the Body

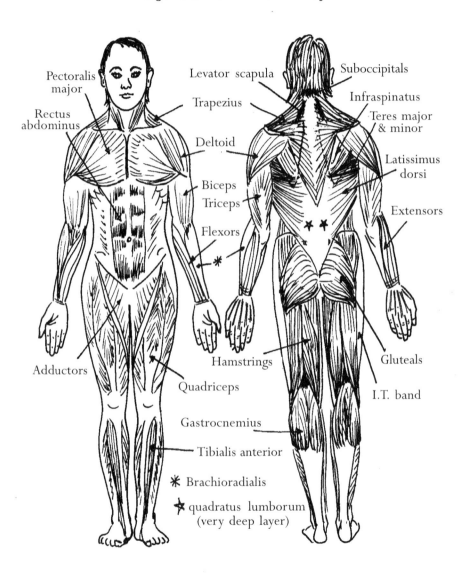

Pectoralis major

Rectus abdominus

Levator scapula

Suboccipitals

Trapezius

Infraspinatus

Teres major & minor

Deltoid

Latissimus dorsi

Biceps

Triceps

Extensors

Flexors

Adductors

Hamstrings

Gluteals

Quadriceps

I.T. band

Gastrocnemius

Tibialis anterior

✳ Brachioradialis

✦ quadratus lumborum
(very deep layer)

Blood Vessels and Nerves of the Body

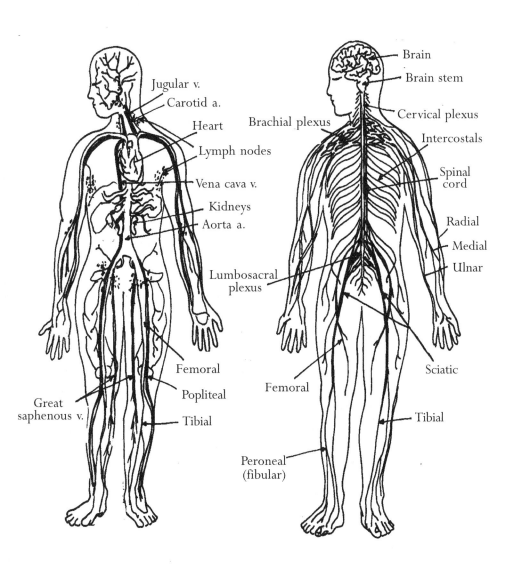

Jugular v.
Carotid a.
Heart
Lymph nodes
Vena cava v.
Kidneys
Aorta a.
Lumbosacral plexus
Femoral
Popliteal
Great saphenous v.
Tibial

Brain
Brain stem
Cervical plexus
Brachial plexus
Intercostals
Spinal cord
Radial
Medial
Ulnar
Femoral
Sciatic
Tibial
Peroneal (fibular)

Eight Ways to Protect Your Health, Your Greatest Wealth

1. Your body is like your personal "pond," and it needs a continual fresh source of pure water (six to eight glasses a day minimum). Your wastes must be promptly and completely removed (from tissues, kidneys, skin, and intestines—especially the bowel). Eat more fiber!

2. Honor your "down" times. Rest. Play. Sleep. If you have an injury, give the tissues total inactivity for a few days. If you have a strain, sprain, or fracture, only immobility will allow the tissues to set properly. Connective tissue needs to patch itself with scar tissue to heal. Then gradually begin movement and strengthening exercises.

3. Your body needs sufficient cellular nutrition or your cells will die. You need nutrient-rich foods, including living foods containing *mana* from the *'āina*, from numerous natural sources. Include power foods like herbs, dark green leafy vegetables, seaweed, miso, bee pollen, legumes, garlic, ginger, sprouts, seeds, good fatty acids, and whole grains.

4. Exercise, move your limbs, and work out your heart. All muscles must be contracted (shortened) as well as stretched (lengthened). This is the *only* way to keep your joints and heart healthy. It is also essential to circulate your lymph fluid, which contains our disease-fighting white blood cells and makes up most of the fluid in our "pond."

5. You must not pollute your body or environment with deadly poisons, chemicals, or toxins. This includes exposing your lungs to smoke, your skin to chemicals, your nerves to excessive stress, your liver to drugs, your vessels to clogging saturated fats, your intestines with putrefying matter, etc.

6. Let go of excessive doubt, worry, fear, resentment, anger, and other negative feelings and thoughts. It is a sure way to weaken you, escalate your pain, and cause more problems.

7. Love yourself. Set healthy boundaries, do service for others, cultivate your intuition, learn from your mistakes, and appreciate your unique qualities. Forgive yourself. Practice being your own best friend.

8. Find, keep, and cultivate your connection with God. Always remember that you contain within you a fragment of the living, loving, eternal essence of the universe. The finite human mind cannot possibly grasp the infinite reality that lies ahead. We may use our free will to align ourselves with it, and create a joyous, eternal existence. Have faith! Put your trust in that which your heart of hearts tells you. Nourish your spirit, and always give thanks!

Glossary

A

'āina: the land, the Mother Earth

aka cord: the invisible, sticky, shadowy connection we can have with people and things that come in contact with us

Akua: God, Almighty God; the Great Spirit

akua 'unihipili: deified spirit

ali'i: of royal blood

alo: front, face, presence, light

aloha: love, affection, compassion; honoring the presence of God's love, mercy, and light; to greet or hail

anela: angel

'aumakua: guardian angel or ancestral guide (can also be a shark, turtle, or an owl that protects the whole family)

H

hā: to breathe, exhale, the breath of life; the number four

hāhā: to palpate; diagnostic touch

haole: foreigner (**Haole:** American or Caucasian)

Hawai'i *nei*: this beloved Hawai'i

heiau: place of Hawaiian worship, temple

ho'o-: prefix usually meaning "to bring about" or "to cause"

ho'okupu: offering

ho'ōla: to cure or heal, to bring life

ho'oponopono: to put right, restore order; mental cleansing, forgiveness

hula: the traditional dance of Hawai'i

huna: small particle; hidden secret

K

ka or *ke:* the (precedes singular nouns)

kai: seawater

kala: forgiveness

kanaka maoli: native Hawaiian person (plural, *kānaka*)

kāne: male

kapu: taboo, off limits

kino: body; physical

L

lā'au lapa'au: herbal medicine

lapa'au: medicine

lomilomi: to rub, knead, press, break up, massage

lū'au: Hawaiian feast

M

mālama pono: taking care (to be) pono

mahalo: thank you

mana: spiritual power, life force (*chi* or *ki* in the Orient)

mana'o: thought, idea, opinion, meaning

menehune: legendary race of night-working "small" Hawaiians (said to have built many rock walls and breakwaters in Hawai'i)

N

nā: the (plural article)

na'au: belly; gut feelings or instincts

O

ola: life, health, well-being

ola loa: long life; completely cured

'ole: absent, lacking, without

'ōlelo: the spoken word

P

pau: finished

piko: connection points to future or previous generations; umbilical, genitals, crown of head

pilikia: trouble, problems, distress

pono: goodness, prosperity, just, fair, righteous

puka: hole

pule: prayer, chant

pu'uwai: heart center; emotions

U

'uhane: soul, spirit, ghost

W

wahine: woman (women, *wāhine*)

wai: freshwater or liquid other than seawater; flowing

wikiwiki: hurry, quick

GLOSSARY: HEALERS, MASTERS, ELDERS

kahu: a guardian, keeper of knowledge, foundation

kahuna: an expert, master, minister, sorcerer (plural, *kāhuna*)

kahuna aloha: one who used rituals to enhance love and attraction between two people

kahuna ʻanāʻanā: sorcerer of black magic

kahuna aʻo: teacher

kahuna hāhā: master diagnostician

kahuna haʻihaʻi iwi: bone-setting expert; also for healing sprains, strains, fractures, etc.

kahuna hoʻohānau: midwife

kahuna hoʻohāpai keiki: expert at helping a woman to conceive

kahuna hoʻokelewaʻa: expert at navigating canoes using the heavens and stars

kahuna hoʻoulu ʻai: expert in agriculture and all aspects of planting

kahuna hoʻounauna: one who sent spirits out on errands

kahuna kāhea: faith healer

kahuna kālai: expert carver; sculptor

kahuna kālai waʻa: canoe builder

kahuna kilokilo: seer; reader of omens from the earth, skies, and stars

kahuna lāʻau lapaʻau: herbal medicine practitioner

kahuna lapaʻau: one who treats, heals, or cures

kahuna pule: minister; literally "prayer expert" (chanting or singing)

kauka: a doctor or physician

kupuna: an elder, grandparent, ancestor (plural, *kūpuna*)

kumu: a teacher; source person

Foreword

1. In traditional Hawaiian healing arts, a client is called a "patient."

2. The native population has declined in numbers drastically since the arrival of the Europeans. Contagious diseases were only one of the causes for this. "Genocide" is the term some Hawaiians use to describe the ongoing practice of foreign "divide and conquer" policies that have reduced and weakened the native population dramatically through various political and cultural means.

Preface

3. The island of Hawai'i, also known as the Big Island, is the largest, youngest, and southernmost island of the chain of Hawaiian Islands. The entire archipelago consists of 6,425 square miles of land (16,640 square kilometers) spread out over 1,000 miles. About 4,028 square miles are located on the eight major islands, which are (from south to north) Hawai'i, Maui, Kaho'olawe, Lāna'i, Moloka'i, O'ahu, Kaua'i, and the small, privately-owned Ni'ihau.

4. In 1975, the *Hōkūlea* voyaging canoe, called a "performance-accurate replica" of the Pacific Ocean canoes of many millenia, left Hawai'i to successfully sail throughout the Polynesian triangle (marked by Hawai'i to the north, Aotearoa, New Zealand, to the southwest, and Rapa Nui, or Easter Island, in the southeast), using only ancient navigational methods. This event opened the way for the "Hawaiian Renaissance," which ushered in a whole new era of Polynesian accomplishment.

Chapter 1

5. Hawai'i Volcanoes National Park (HVNP) in the southeast area of the island of Hawai'i, the location of the active volcano of Kīlauea (known as the world's most active volcano), is currently over the "hot spot" of the mid-Pacific Ocean floor. HVNP has grown by 560 acres since 1983 (not counting the huge recent joint acquisition of 116,000 acres of Kahuku Ranch with the financial and political help of the Nature

Conservancy), when it began its latest "active eruption" phase. The park, which is a haven for artists, writers, and hikers, is the second largest tourist attraction of the entire Hawaiian Islands. Park employees conduct ongoing educational programs and eliminate many alien plant species in order to preserve the park's unique endemic forests.

6. *Poi*, which is made by mashing *taro*, is the pudding-like carbohydrate staple of the Hawaiian peoples. The very growing and eating of *taro* has always been symbolic of the sustaining gift of life from the sacred earth to each of her people, generation after generation. In the nineteenth century, when the Hawaiian language became a written language, a lot of the consonants changed, making it different from the rest of Polynesia. For example, the *k* replaced the *t*, and the *l* replaced the *r*; thus *tahuna* became *kahuna*, *aroha* became *aloha*, and *taro* became *kalo*. Yet *taro* and *ti* are today most often called by their original names.

7. Internal cleansing refers primarily to the colon or large intestine, but can also include the entire gastro-intestinal tract, as well as the blood and lymphatics via the circulatory and urinary systems.

8. The Bishop P. Museum was founded in 1889 after Bernice Pauahi Bishop, the last descendant of the royal Kamehameha family. It houses millions of Hawaiian cultural artifacts, archive documents, and royal heir-looms, and runs a press, ethnobotanical garden, and bookstore. www.bishopmuseum.org

9. The last monarch of the Kingdom of Hawai'i before its illegal overthrow was Queen Lili'uokalani, today well known for her grace, devotion to her people, and beautiful songs, including the famous *Aloha 'Oe*. Although she officially reigned for only two years (1891-1893), she is still very respected and dearly beloved by the people of Hawai'i.

Chapter 3

10. The four primary post-Tahitian Gods were Kāne, Lono, Kū, and Kanaloa. Kāne's full name was Kanenuiakea, and there were many Kāne stones known as "gateways to heaven" in every *ahupua'a* where one could ask for refuge, forgiveness, and blessings. Lono and Kū were a part of Kāne; they each are the *'aumakua* in the geneology of their respective orders of priesthoods. Lono is associated with healing, agriculture, and the annual *makahiki* festivities. Kū (Tū) is associated with the depths of the ocean (the origins of life as in the *Kumulipo* creation chant) and also sacrifice and warfare; Kanaloa with water and the ocean, the very essence of life on Earth.

Chapter 4

11. Pele and Poli'ahu are the names of two energetic, opposing elements of the volcanoes. Pele is wild, intense, and raw. She is known as the goddess representing fire, which destroys and also creates land and life. Poli'ahu is the cooler, calmer, and gentler goddess. She is seen and felt by many sensitive souls throughout the year, but expecially when the blankets of snow grace Mauna Kea (and occasionally Mauna Loa) during the winter months, gently reflecting the moonlight.

12. The breath of life, known as *hā*, was (and is) very sacred in Hawai'i. This was the means by which sacred knowledge and great *mana* was passed from an elder to another person.

Chapter 6

13. The 24 canoe "migration plants" are *'ape, 'awa, 'awapuhi kuahiwi, hau, ipu, kalo, kamani, kī, kō, kou, kukui, mai'a, milo, niu, noni, 'ohe, 'ōhi'a 'ai, 'olena, olona, pia, 'uala, uhi, 'ulu,* and *waike.*

14. Gutmanis, June (various writings)

15. Kaiahua, Kalua (various writings)

16. Gutmanis

17. Kaiahua

18. Krauss, Beatrice (various writings)

19. Kaiahua

20. Keliihoomalu, Robert Sr. (oral)

21. Krauss

22. Gutmanis

23. Auwae, Henry (oral)

24. Krauss

25. Kaiahua

26. Gutmanis

27. Kaiahua

28. Kaiahua

29. Keliihoomalu

30. Auwae

31. Gutmanis

32. Gutmanis

33. Kaiahua

34. Fragas, Mary (oral)

35. Kaiahua

36. Keliihoomalu

37. Keliihoomalu

38. Gutmanis

39. Gutmanis

40. Kaiahua

41. Gutmanis and Keliihoomalu

42. Machado, Margaret (oral)

Chapter 7

43. *Lehua* blossoms are the bright red (occasionally whitish-yellow) flowers of the native *'ōhi'a* tree, the first tree to emerge from new lava flows, which blanket the volcanic Puna district.

Becker, Catherine Kalama, Ph.D. *Mana Cards.* Publisher: Radiance Network, Inc. ISBN# 0-9660142-0-0.

Chun, Malcolm Naea. *Must We Wait In Despair: 1867 Report of the 'Ahahui Lā'au Lapa'au.* Publisher: First People's Productions, 1994.

Dougherty, Michael. *To Steal a Kingdom: Probing Hawaiian History.* Publisher: Island Style Press. ISBN# 0-96334840X.

Gutmanis, June. *Kahuna Lā'au Lapa'au.* Publisher: Island Heritage Publishing. ISBN# 0-89610-078-2.

Handy, E. S. Craighill, Mary Kawena Pukui, and Katherine Livermore. *Outline of Hawaiian Physical Therapeutics* (Bulletin 126). Publisher: Bishop Museum, 1934. Reprinted by Kraus Reprint Co., 1971.

Harden, M. J. and Steve Brinkman. *Voices of Wisdom: Hawaiian Elders Speak.* Publisher: Aka Press. ISBN# 0-944134-01-7.

I'i, John Papa and Mary Kawena Pukui. *Fragments of Hawaiian History.* Publisher: Bishop Museum Press, 1963.

Juvik, Sonia P., and James O., Editors. *Atlas of Hawaii.* Publisher: University of Hawai'i Press, Honolulu, 1998. ISBN# 0-8248-2125-4.

Kaiahua, Kalua. *Hawaiian Healing Herbs.* Publisher: Ka'imi Pono Press. ISBN# 0-9643829-4-6.

Kamakau, Samuel Manaiakalani. *Ka Mo 'olelo Hawai'i: The People of Old.* Publisher: Bishop Museum Press. ISBN# 0-910240-32-9.

King, Serge Kahili, Ph.D. *Kahuna Healing.* Publisher: Theosophical Publishing. ISBN# 0-8356-0572-8.

Krauss, Beatrice H. *Native Plants Used as Medicine in Hawaii.* Publisher: Lyon Arboretum, 1981.

Lee, Pali J. and John Koko Willis. *Children of the Night Rainbow.* ISBN# 0-9628030-0-6.

Lee, Pali J. and John Koko Willis. *Ho'opono* (out of print).

Long, Max Freedom. *The Secret Science Behind Miracles.* Publisher: DeVorss & Company. ISBN# 0-87516-047-6.

Malo, David. *Hawaiian Antiquities* (second edition). Publisher: Bishop Museum Press, 1951.

McBride, L. R. *The Kahuna: Versatile Mystics of Old Hawaii.* Publisher: The Petroglyph Press. ISBN# 0-912180-18-8.

Pukui, Mary Kawena. *Nana I Ke Kumu: Look to the Source.* Publisher: Hui Hanai. ISBN# 0-916630-13-7 (vol. 1) and ISBN# 0-916630-14-5 (vol. 2).

Pukui, Mary Kawena. *'ŌLELO NO'EAU: Hawaiian Proverbs & Poetical Sayings.* Publisher: Bishop Museum Press. ISBN# 0-910240-93-0.

Pukui, Mary Kawena and Samuel H. Elbert. *New Pocket Hawaiian Dictionary.* Publisher: University of Hawai'i Press, 1992. ISBN# 0-8248-1392-8.

Scott, Greg. *Journey to Kanaka Makua: Pacific Voyager Cards.* Self-Published: PO Box 1722, Keaau, HI. 96749.

Sherwood, Zelie D. *Beginner's Hawaiian.* Publisher: Ku Pa'a Publishing, Inc. ISBN# 0-914916-56-4.

Taylor, Clarice B. *Hawaiian Almanac.* Publisher: Mutual Publishing. ISBN# 1-56647-114-1.

Yates, Maka'ala, DC. *The Ideal Health Manual: A Healthy Alternative Way of Life.* Publisher: Mana Ola Enterprises, 1998.

For those of you online, check these sites for some possible referrals and useful information:

www.BigIslandMassage.com
www.lomilomi.org
www.HawaiianHealingInstitute.com
www.lomilomi.biz
www.kohala.net/kaimalino
www.hawaiian.net/〜kea/aunty.html
www.huna.org
www.mapunawaiola.com
www.ulukau.org
www.kalama.org
www.lokahiola.org
www.lomilomi.com
www.canoeplants.com
www.HaleOla.com
www.LomiHawaii.com

About the Author

Nancy S. Kahalewai moved to Hawai'i from California in 1973 after studying fine arts at Pasadena City College. She was drawn to the healing arts and received her Hawai'i massage license in 1977. She was one of the founding members of Ke Ola Hou, a health-education center in Hilo from 1975 to 1982.

She has two half-Hawaiian sons and two part-Hawaiian grandchildren. Over the years, she became very involved with the Hawaiian culture. She and her family lived on the Kona coast from 1982 to 1989, where she founded the Hawaiian Islands School of Body Therapies and ran massage clinics at both the 'Ohana Keauhou Beach Hotel and King Kamehameha Kona Beach Hotel. During this time she met *lomilomi* master Aunty Margaret Machado, *kahuna* Daddy Bray, Jr., and studied many massage modalities, including *lomilomi,* athletic massage, and many specialty techniques. She codirected the finish line massage team for the Ironman World Championship Triathlon in Kona for seven years, and met such healing arts pioneers as Judith Aston, Milton

Trager, Robert King, John Harris, Robert Calvert, and Deepak Chopra, MD.

In 1992, she returned to Hilo and studied human biology and athletic training at the University of Hawai'i at Hilo. She also took advanced anatomy classes from other massage pioneers, including Myk Hungerford, Tom Meyers, and Deane Juhan. She became NCBTMB certified in 1994, directed the Volcano Marathon massage team for five years, and studied *lomilomi* and *lāʻau lapaʻau* with a number of Hawaiian teachers and elders. During this time, she founded her second school, the Big Island Academy of Massage, which she sold in 2003. Her graduates now practice throughout the United States, Canada, and Japan.

She is the CEO of I. M. Publishing, a print-on-demand publishing company in Hawai'i. She also teaches *lomilomi* and human anatomy. She is writing a new book on Uncle Robert Keliihoomalu's memoirs of old Kalapana, and archiving major Hawaiian sovereignty and healing arts events from the 1990s to the present. She has a private practice in aromatherapy, reflexology, and Hawaiian massage. In her spare time she kayaks, dances salsa, and rides her Harley-Davidson motorcycle.

Contact her by e-mail at: mail@bigislandmassage.com.

To order signed copies of this book, please contact the publisher at: info@IslandMoonlight.com.

CPSIA information can be obtained at www.ICGtesting.com
Printed in the USA
BVOW08s0958300716

457252BV00008B/2/P

9 780967 725321